IELTS Advantage

Speaking &
Listening Skills

Jon Marks

DELTA Publishing
Quince Cottage
Hoe Lane
Peaslake
Surrey GU5 9SW
England

www.deltapublishing.co.uk

First published 2013

Edited by Catriona Watson-Brown
Designed by Caroline Johnston
Photos by Bigstock (page 11 (both))
    Stock.XCHNG (pages 15 (both), 21 (right), 26 (top right, bottom),
    31 (both), 41 (left), 51 (both), 53 (all), 61 (left), 64, 71 (both),
    73 (credit: Mei Teng), 77 (left: Kate Krav; right: Garwee), 102)
    Shutterstock (pages 13, 17 (all), 26 (left))
    iStock (pages 21 (left), 29, 32, 41 (right), 45, 55, 61 (right), 62,
    85 (both), 87, 89, 91, 95 (both), 96, 98)
    Thinkstock (page 46)
Illustrations (pages 92 and 93) by Kathy Baxendale
Cartoons by CartoonStock (pages 19, 48, 78, 88, 100)
Cover design by Peter Bushell
Printed in China by RR Donnelley

ISBN Book 978-1-905085-64-4

Author acknowledgements
Thanks to: Nick Boisseau at Delta Publishing for captaining the ship;
Catriona Watson-Brown for editing; Alison Wooder for checking the
first draft; the other authors of the *IELTS Advantage* series for cross-
fertilization of ideas, and in particular Richard Brown for helpful
comments on the initial proposal for this volume; my IELTS students
over the years, many of whom worked with earlier versions of material
in this book.

Contents

SPEAKING

LISTENING

CD track list

Track 1: Unit 1, Listen 1 (Speaking Part 1)

Track 2: Unit 1, Listen 2 (Speaking Part 1)

Track 3: Unit 2, Listen 1 (Speaking Part 1)

Track 4: Unit 2, Listen 2 (Speaking Part 1)

Track 5: Unit 3, Listen 1 (Speaking Part 2)

Track 6: Unit 3, Listen 2 (Speaking Part 3)

Track 7: Unit 4, Listen 1 (Speaking Part 2)

Track 8: Unit 4, Listen 2 (Speaking Part 3)

Track 9: Unit 5, Listen 1 (Speaking Part 2)

Track 10: Unit 5, Listen 2 (Speaking Part 3)

Track 11: Unit 6, Listen 1 (Speaking Part 2)

Track 12: Unit 6, Listen 2 (Speaking Part 3)

Track 13: Unit 7, Listen 1 (Speaking Part 2)

Track 14: Unit 7, Listen 2 (Speaking Part 3)

Track 15: Unit 8 (Listening Section 1, four extracts)

Track 16: Unit 8 (Listening Section 1, full-length)

Track 17: Unit 8 (Listening Section 2, three extracts)

Track 18: Unit 8 (Listening Section 2, full-length)

Track 19: Unit 8 (Listening Section 2, full-length)*

Track 20: Unit 8 (Listening Section 2, full-length)

Track 21: Unit 8 (Listening Section 2, full-length)*

Track 22: Unit 9 (Listening Section 3, extract)

Track 23: Unit 9 (Listening Section 3, full-length)*

Track 24: Unit 9 (Listening Section 4, extract)

Track 25: Unit 9 (Listening Section 4, full-length)*

* In the IELTS test, there is a sufficient pause to allow students to read the questions. The recordings on this CD need to be paused at the relevant point(s) to enable students to do this.

Introduction

Aim of the book

IELTS Advantage Speaking & Listening Skills is designed for students who want to achieve a score of 6.5–7.0 or higher in the Speaking and Listening modules of the Academic IELTS exam. The majority of candidates aim to get at least 6.5, in order to study at university, to work abroad, to apply for a visa or to have proof of a good level of English. The book aims to develop your speaking and listening skills up to and beyond this level. Companion volumes in this series are *IELTS Advantage Writing Skills* and *IELTS Advantage Reading Skills*.

The book is divided into two sections: Speaking and Listening.
The content of the Speaking section has five main features:

- Format explanations and exam tips to help you predict and prepare for the Speaking test
- Grammar, vocabulary, collocations and expressions relating to the common themes and topics featured in the Speaking test
- Exam skills and strategies for the Speaking test
- Plentiful opportunities to practise speaking in the format of the Speaking test
- Audio examples on the accompanying CD of model Speaking tests

The content of the Listening section has three main features:

- Format explanations and exam tips to help you predict and prepare for the Listening test
- Development of strategies for listening and extracting the information necessary to answer the questions
- Listening practice material based on the accompanying CD

Using this book in the classroom

Each unit comprises around 90–120 minutes of classroom material. The lessons can be taught as a short stand-alone course of around 20 to 30 hours, or can be used as supplementary material.

Using this book for self study

This book has much to offer as a self-study resource. The exam tips and explanations, the language-practice activities and the audio material on the CD will provide a thorough preparation for the Speaking and Listening tests. To get the best from the speaking activities, work with a 'study buddy'. For most of these activities, one person plays the role of the examiner and the other plays the role of the candidate. Then you reverse roles and repeat.

Organization of the book

- Units 1 and 2: These focus on Speaking Part 1. In this part of the Speaking test, the examiner asks the candidate questions about familiar topics relating to his/her life.
- Units 3 to 7: These have an introductory section based on Speaking Part 1, followed by the main focus on Speaking Parts 2 and 3. In these parts of the test, the candidate prepares and delivers a short talk (Part 2), then discusses related topics further with the examiner (Part 3).
- Units 8 and 9: Listening

Some features of the Speaking section

- **Try it first!**

  Before you start each section, you are encouraged to role-play speaking on the topic of the unit as if in the test. This can help to show you the strong and weak points of your speaking, so you can see how you need to improve.

- **Spotlight**

  Explanation and practice of grammar, vocabulary, collocations and expressions which are particularly useful for talking about the topics of the unit and for answering the kinds of question typically asked in the Speaking test.

- **Exam skills**

  Skills and strategies for improving the quality of your replies to the examiner's questions. These will help you to give more complex answers which fully demonstrate your ability to use English.

- **Prepare and practise**

  Activities for organizing and developing your ideas so you will have plenty to say on the topics. These are followed by a role-play speaking on the topic as if in the exam, aiming to use language learned in the unit as much as possible.

- **Listen**

  Listen to extracts from the Speaking test. Compare the model with your version in order to learn further useful ideas and strategies.

- **Pronunciation focus**

  Tasks and suggestions for improving this essential aspect of spoken English.

- **Tips**

  Extra advice and information for improving your performance on the day of the test.

- **Check and challenge**

  Activities which review the content of the unit, plus suggestions for further study and skills development.

- **Four practice Speaking test role-plays**

  Four full-length Speaking tests covering other topics which commonly appear in the exam. These give additional opportunities to practise speaking, and further demonstrate the structure of the test.

Some features of the Listening section

Explanations, advice, strategy ideas and practice relating to all the formats of the Listening test:

- Multiple choice
- Matching
- Completing sentences
- Completing tables
- Completing forms
- Completing notes
- Writing short answers
- Completing summaries
- Completing flow charts
- Labelling maps/diagrams

About the Speaking test

Structure

- **Part 1:** The examiner asks general questions about familiar subjects such as your home, family, free-time interests and occupation or studies. It's common for the examiner to begin with questions relating to the practical side of your personal life, and then to move on to your leisure interests and/or other experiences of everyday life.
- **Part 2:** The examiner gives you a card with instructions to talk about a topic for up to two minutes. You have a minute to prepare, and can make notes if you wish. After the talk, the examiner may ask one or two 'rounding-off' questions about the topic.
- **Part 3:** The examiner asks further questions which develop the topic of Part 2 and generate a conversation featuring more abstract ideas and issues related to the topic of Part 2.

The total length is 11 to 14 minutes, and the whole interview is recorded.

During the test

IELTS examiners are thoroughly trained to give standard conditions in the tests. They are assessing your ability to communicate effectively, and you will not usually lose marks for minor errors or hesitations. It's normal to feel nervous before the test, and the examiner will try to help you feel more relaxed. He/She will talk to you in a friendly and informal manner, and will not try to trick you into making mistakes.

In simple terms, the Speaking test starts easy and gradually becomes more difficult. However, that doesn't mean that you shouldn't aim to give complex answers in Part 1. The examiner works from a printed set of questions, but has some flexibility to ask additional questions in order to discover the extent of your English ability as accurately as possible.

You should try to give your ideas and opinions, but will be assessed solely on the quality of your English, not your knowledge of the topic or your personal views. The examiner will not ask you directly about politics or religion. You can refer to those if you wish (provided they are relevant to the question), but you are recommended to avoid topics which make you feel emotional, as this may distract you from giving your best possible performance in English.

What are the examiners looking for?

The IELTS examiners are assessing several different things, and this book is designed to help you in each of these areas:

- **Vocabulary**
  You need to have a good range of words and phrases relating to the typical topics featured in the test. Unlike the Writing test, it's not necessary to use formal, academic English. Standard conversational English is acceptable. You will gain marks for good use of collocations (or 'word partnerships'), fixed expressions and words and phrases for linking ideas.
- **Grammar**
  You need to use grammar accurately. To get a high score, you need to show you can use a range of complex structures for purposes such as describing relationships between the past, present and future, and describing relationships of cause and effect. A common mistake made by candidates is to answer using simple and repetitive grammar rather than showing they can use more complex language.
- **Organization**
  You need to speak in a clear, well-organized way and give answers which are easy to follow. The structure is not quite as important as it is in the Writing test, but you will gain marks for presenting your ideas in a well-structured way. A common mistake, especially in Part 2, is to give ideas which lack structure and a clear purpose.

- **Ideas and arguments**

  You need to communicate complex and well-developed ideas and to answer the questions fully and with clear points of view. Common mistakes are failing to answer the examiner's question properly, and giving answers which don't go into enough detail to demonstrate a high level of English.

- **Pronunciation**

  The accuracy of your pronunciation is very important. Speaking with a non-native accent is not a problem, but the examiner will assess how easy it is for a listener to understand your pronunciation.

- **Speed**

  If you speak too fast, it will make what you say difficult to follow, especially if you also make some language and pronunciation errors. If you speak too slowly, it may suggest that you need too much thinking time for normal conversation. It may also mean you don't have enough time to demonstrate your English fully.

The above features are often summarized as:
- fluency and coherence (general ability to communicate effectively)
- lexical resource (vocabulary)
- grammatical range and accuracy
- pronunciation.

About the Listening test

Structure

There are four sections, each comprising ten questions. You get one mark for each correct answer.
- **Section 1:** a conversation between two people in an everyday social situation
- **Section 2:** a monologue in an everyday social context
- **Section 3:** a conversation between two (or occasionally more than two) people in an education or training situation
- **Section 4:** a talk or lecture in an academic style on a subject of general interest

The test lasts for approximately 30 minutes, followed by ten minutes for transferring answers to the answer sheet. Each part of the recording is played only once.

What are the examiners looking for?

The test is designed to assess your skills in several different areas, including:
- listening for the gist
- listening for the main points
- listening for detailed information
- listening to understand a complex idea or argument
- listening to infer the opinion of a speaker
- listening to make deductions about an unfamiliar topic
- listening to make deductions despite not understanding all the words.

The IELTS scoring system

IELTS exam scores go up in steps of 0.5 from 1.0 to 9.0. A score of 9.0 is considered to be very near native-speaker level. However, as the tasks are difficult and the time is limited, even native speakers are not guaranteed to get a score of 9.0. It's rare for a non-native speaker to get more than 8.0, and very few organizations and institutions require a score of more than 7.5.

The Common European Framework of languages (CEF) categorizes IELTS scores as follows:

level	CEF	IELTS
Upper-intermediate	B2	5.0/5.5/6.0
Advanced	C1	6.5/7.0
Upper-advanced/Proficiency	C2	7.5+

Here is a guide to what you can normally do with these scores. However, be sure to check with the employer or educational institution you are applying to.

- 5.5–6.0 Entry to a university Foundation course
- 6.0–6.5 Entry to a Bachelor's degree course
- 6.5–7.0 Entry to a Master's degree course
- 7.0+ Typically required to work in English-speaking countries in professions such as medicine, law and accounting

Personal circumstances

SPEAKING PART 1: OCCUPATIONS

In Part 1 of the Speaking test, the examiner asks you some general questions about your personal situation. These may include questions about your occupation (or the way you spend your time if you don't have an occupation). It's a good idea to prepare some ideas for speaking about this. What can you say that is interesting or unexpected? Can you give some opinions as well as the basic information?

Try it first!

Try talking about your occupation as if you were doing Speaking Part 1. If you are working with a partner, take it in turns to play the roles of examiner and candidate. Here are some typical questions.

Examiner: I'd like to ask you some questions about your occupation.

- Do you work, or are you a student?
- What's the most interesting part of being a [*candidate's occupation*]?
- What's the most difficult part of being a [*candidate's occupation*]?
- Would you say it's a good occupation? (Why? / Why not?)
- What kind of work would you like to do in the future?

Spotlight 1
Useful language for talking about your occupation

Grammar: present simple or present continuous?

Your choice of grammar shows how you feel about your occupation.

Present simple
I **work** for a company which makes car engine parts.
This implies you feel the job is long term.

Present continuous
I**'m working** for a company which makes car engine parts.
This implies you feel the job is temporary.

If you're a student, it's common to use the present continuous to describe your course:
I**'m doing** a Master's degree in Forest Management.

1 Choose the best sentence from each pair.

1 a I study Chemistry at the local university.
  b I'm studying Chemistry at the local university.
2 a I don't work at the moment.
  b I'm not working at the moment.
3 a My family owns a chain of opticians, and I run one of the branches.
  b My family is owning a chain of opticians, and I'm running one of the branches.

Vocabulary: prepositions with *work*

2 Choose the best preposition to complete each of these sentences.

1 I work *to / for* a marketing company.
2 I work *in / at* advertising.
3 I'm working *of / at* the local library.
4 I work *by / with* some interesting people.
5 I'm working *on / about* a very interesting project at the moment.
6 I work *as / at* a theatrical lighting designer.

Vocabulary: expressions connected with work

3 Complete the sentences below giving opinions about occupations using the expressions in the box.

career prospects	job satisfaction	job security
paid by the hour	physically demanding	work long hours

1 Doctors often have to ....
2 I work in a restaurant, and I don't have a regular salary. I'm ....
3 I love seeing children learn. That's why I get so much .... from being a teacher.
4 I don't work for any one newspaper. I'm a freelance journalist. That means I have no ....
5 In sales, you can start at the bottom and work your way to the top. It's a job with excellent ....
6 I'm a road mender. My job mostly involves filling holes in the road. It's tiring and .... work.

Tip
There are many fixed expressions in English. Learning and using them can make your English seem more 'natural', and will help improve your score in both the Speaking and Writing tests.

Exam skills 1

Giving plenty of detail in descriptions

Don't just say *I'm a student* or *I work in a restaurant*. Give more details in your answer. For example:

- *I'm a third-year student studying Law at the local university.*
- *I'm working as a waiter in a pizza restaurant in the main square of this town. You may have seen it. It's called Pappagallo.*

The examiner may ask for your opinion or feelings about your occupation. It can be a good strategy to contrast a positive and a negative opinion. For example:

- *It's not an easy subject. There's a lot of reading, and the exams are very difficult, but it'll be worth it.*
- *I'll be able to get a good job when I graduate, and the career prospects for lawyers are excellent.*
- *It's hard work and – I have to be honest – the pay isn't great, but it can be a lot of fun, especially when the restaurant is busy. I work with some really nice people.*

Tip
Adding your feelings and opinions can make your speaking more interesting and can help improve your score. However, extreme and intolerant opinions should be avoided, especially concerning race and religion.

1 **Write a description of your occupation. Include some suitable opinions/feelings.**

Language check

2 **Look at your description from Exercise 1. What tenses have you used? Can you change them to include more advanced tenses? Can you change the vocabulary to include some more advanced words and phrases?**

Examples:

... the exams are very difficult. ➔ *... the exams are really tough.*

I meet lots of interesting people. ➔ *I've met lots of memorable characters.*

Prepare and practise

Tip
You won't be able to write notes in Part 1 of the exam (you can in Part 2), but doing it now will help you to organize your ideas.

3 **Prepare your ideas for speaking about your occupation. Write some brief notes on ways to answer these questions. Can you use the ideas in Spotlight 1 (page 12) and above?**

- Do you work, or are you a student?
- What's the most interesting part of being a [*candidate's occupation*]?
- What's the most difficult part of being a [*candidate's occupation*]?
- Would you say it's a good occupation? (Why? / Why not?)
- What kind of work would you like to do in the future?

Tip
Although it's a good strategy to prepare your ideas and learn useful language, don't memorize a speech and then give it in the test. What you say should seem spontaneous.

4 **If you are working with a partner, role-play talking about your occupations as if in Part 1 of the Speaking test again – one person is the examiner and the other is the candidate. Use the same sample questions, and refer to the notes you made in Exercise 3 if you wish to. When you have finished, reverse roles and repeat.**

5 **Write a detailed description of your occupation. Use a dictionary to describe it as accurately as you can. This will help you to organize your ideas and to learn new words that will be useful.**

Listen 1

1 🎧 **1** **Listen to the recording, which is based on Speaking Part 1. Answer each of these questions using no more than TWO WORDS.**

    1 The candidate is doing a degree in ....

    2 He is also working as a ....

    3 The most interesting part of the job is conversations with the ....

    4 The most difficult part is dealing with some of the parents of children who
    ....

    5 In the future, he wants to work in a ....

2 **Now look at the audio transcript on page 105 and check your answers.**

3 **Was the recording very different from your role-play (Exercise 4, page 13)? How was it different? How could you improve further? Discuss your ideas with a partner or in small groups. Think about these areas:**

    1 Did you have plenty of things to say?

    2 Were your ideas joined together in a logical sequence?

    3 Did you use the best possible vocabulary?

    4 Did you use the best possible grammar?

    5 Did you speak in a relaxed and confident way without a lot of hesitation?

    6 Was your pronunciation good?

Pronunciation focus: sentence stress

🎧 **1** Listen to the beginning of the recording again. Notice how some words in the sentence are stressed. For example:

I'm also working as a **lifeguard** *at my local* **swimming pool**.

In this case, *lifeguard* and *swimming pool* are the most important words, so they are stressed the most. *Working* and *local* are less important, so they have less stress. The other words (*I'm also ... as a ... at my ...*) are words which the listener can almost guess from the context, so they receive the least stress of all.

4 🎧 **1** **Listen to the whole recording again while reading the audio transcript on page 105. While you listen, underline the most important words in the candidate's responses – the words which are stressed the most. Then practise saying these sentences with the underlined words stressed.**

> **Tip**
> The examiner will consider your pronunciation when deciding the grade to award you. You will not be expected to sound like a native speaker to get a high score, but of course it is a good idea to improve your pronunciation as much as you can.

5 **Work in pairs, asking each other the questions below. Again, one person is the examiner, the other is the candidate. When you have finished, reverse roles and repeat. Try to include improvements you noticed when you listened to the recording, and try to improve your use of sentence stress.**

- Describe the place where you work or study.
- How long have you worked/studied there?
- What do you like about this place?
- How do you usually travel there?
- What changes would improve your journey there?

SPEAKING PART 1: PLACES OF RESIDENCE

Another common topic in Part 1 of the Speaking test is personal circumstances – the place where you live, your family and your daily life. As with your occupation, it's a good idea to prepare some ideas to talk about. What can you say about these topics that is interesting or unexpected? Can you give some opinions as well as the basic information?

Try it first!

Try talking about the place where you live as if you were doing Speaking Part 1. If you are working with a partner, take it in turns to play the roles of examiner and candidate. Here are some typical questions.

Examiner: I'd like to talk about the place where you live.

- Can you describe the building you live in?
- Is it similar to other buildings in the area?
- Is it a convenient location for you?
- What do you like about living there?
- What changes would improve the area where you live?

Spotlight 2

Useful language for talking about your place of residence

Grammar: present perfect or present perfect continuous?

Your choice of grammar should reflect whether your living situation is permanent, long term or temporary.

Present perfect (permanent or long term)
*I've **lived** in this city all my life.*
*My family **has lived** in this area since my grandparents moved here in about 1950.*
*I've **lived** in the same house for 15 years. I think it's time to move.*

Present perfect continuous (temporary)
*I've **been staying** with friends for the last few weeks.*
*I've only **been living** here since last Tuesday.*
*I've **been looking** for somewhere to live which is closer to work.*

However, with *live* for longer-term but non-permanent situations, often both forms are possible.

*I've **lived** in university accommodation for the last two years.*
*I've **been living** in university accommodation for the last two years.*

The second version emphasises that the situation is not permanent, but these two versions could be interchangeable in many situations.

Natural English: *be* **instead of** *live*
It's common to use a form of the verb *to be* to imply *live.*
I'm in rented accommodation at the moment.
I've been in a college residence since I started my course.
We're on the seventh floor.

1 Look at these pairs of sentences. Which version is better? Or are both good?

1 a I've lived here since I was two years old.
   b I've been living here since I was two years old.
2 a I've lived here for quite a long time.
   b I've been living here for quite a long time.
3 a I've lived with my parents since I graduated last year.
   b I've been living with my parents since I graduated last year.
4 a I live very near the city centre.
   b I'm very near the city centre.
5 a I've lived in several different places.
   b I've been living in several different places.

2 Present perfect or present perfect continuous? Complete each gap with the correct form of the verb in brackets.

1 It's the nicest place I've ever .... (*live*)
2 I haven't .... very many other places. (*see*)
3 We've .... of moving for a few months now. (*think*)
4 I've never .... in rented accommodation. (*live*)
5 I haven't .... a new place for very long. (*look for*)
6 I've never .... in a university residence before. (*stay*)
7 I've just .... a really nice apartment. (*find*)
8 We still haven't found the kind of place we've .... to find. (*hope*)

Vocabulary: places of residence

3 **Do these adjectives usually describe houses/flats or areas/neighbourhoods? Write them in the correct column of the table below.**

commercial   fourth-floor   multicultural   rented
residential   rural   shared   spacious
suburban   three-storey   two-bedroom   urban

house/flat	area/neighbourhood

4 **Complete these sentences with words/phrases from Exercise 3.**

1 This part of the city is very .... There are wonderful shops and cafés from all around the world.
2 You wouldn't call my flat .... It's like living in a cupboard.
3 Not many people live in the .... district. It's mostly shops and offices.
4 It's very .... where I live. We're at least 30 kilometres from the nearest town.
5 It's nice to have your own place, but it's usually much cheaper to live in a .... house or flat.
6 To get to the city centre, you go past kilometre after kilometre of dull .... housing.

British or American English?

5 **Both British and American English are acceptable in the exam, but it is best to be consistent. In each pair, which term is American English (AE) and which is British English (BE)?**

1 lift / elevator
2 apartment / flat
3 ground floor / first floor
4 sidewalk / pavement
5 crossroads / intersection
6 main road / highway
7 downtown / town centre

Exam skills 2

Combining details to give complex answers

The examiner can direct the conversation into related areas. So for example, a first question about the place where you live could lead to questions about the people you live with and your daily routine at home. You should include plenty of information and your feelings/opinions. For example:

I share a small flat with two other students. It's not very convenient for the city centre, but it's cheap and it's near the university where I'm studying at the moment.

1 Write notes for each of these topics, then expand them to give your feelings/opinions about them.

your home (flat, house, etc.)	family and/or people you live with	daily routine at home
small flat	share with two other students	

Prepare and practise

2 On a separate piece of paper, write a complex answer to each of the questions below, combining at least three pieces of information for each one. (This includes questions which could be answered with just *Yes/No*.)

Example:

Q: Do you still live there?

A: Yes, I do. Most of my family and friends live in the area, and one reason I chose to study at my local university was so I wouldn't have to find a place to live somewhere else.

1 Describe the village, town or city where you grew up.
2 Do you still live there?
3 Does your family still live there?
4 How much has it changed since you were young?
5 Do you like living there? (Why? / Why not?)
6 Describe the street or area you live in.
7 Do you think it's a good place to live? (Why? / Why not?)
8 How well do you know the people who live next door to you?
9 What are the advantages of knowing your neighbours well?
10 What kind of problems can people have with their neighbours?

3 Work in pairs. One person is the examiner, the other is the candidate. The examiner asks questions 1–5 from Exercise 2. Then reverse roles and repeat with questions 6–10. Refer to the answers you wrote.

Tip
Take an active role in the dialogue, giving extra ideas and information. However, it's not a social conversation. Don't ask the examiner questions.

4 Repeat, but reverse roles, so that the person who asked questions 1–5 the first time now answers them, and vice versa. This time, don't refer to the questions you wrote – try to include all the information from memory.

Listen 2

1 🎧 **2** **Listen to the recording, which is based on Speaking Part 1. Which THREE things are true about the candidate?**

   1 She lives on the eighth floor of an apartment block.
   2 She lives near the city centre.
   3 She's a student.
   4 She has to spend a long time travelling every day.
   5 She thinks the city is a good place to live.
   6 She thinks the worst thing about her city is the cold weather.

2 **Now look at the audio transcript on page 105 and check your answers.**

3 **Was the recording very different from your role-play (Exercises 3 and 4, page 18)? How was it different? How could you improve further? Discuss your ideas with a partner or in small groups.**

Pronunciation focus: connected speech

> 🎧 **2** Listen to the recording again. Notice how many words run into each other, especially the words in frequently used sequences. For example:
>
> *I'm studying_at_a college on the_other_side_of_the city centre, so I spend_about two_hours on_the_bus every day.*
>
> In this example, the words connected with underscores are said almost as if they were just one word:
>
> *studying_at_a*
> *the_other_side_of_the*
> *spend_about*
> *two_hours*
> *on_the_bus*

4 🎧 **2** **Listen to the recording again while reading the audio transcript on page 105. While you listen, underline examples of connected speech in the candidate's responses. Then practise saying these sentences, copying the connected speech as much as you can.**

5 **Work in pairs, asking each other the questions below. Again, one person is the examiner, the other is the candidate. When you have finished, reverse roles and repeat. Try to include improvements you noticed when you listened to the recording, and try to improve your use of connected speech.**

- Describe your home.
- How long have you lived there?
- Which is your favourite room for relaxing in?
- How do you spend the evenings when you are at home?
- What changes would improve your home?

Like it?

FOR SALE

www.CartoonStock.com

Check and challenge

Talking about your occupation

CHECK   **Find language in this unit which is another way to say:**

1 monthly pay cheque
2 pleasure that can come from working
3 self-employed, working for several different clients

CHALLENGE   **Write a short description of your occupation in your first language. Include your feelings about it. Then translate it into English. Ideally, use an English–English dictionary.**

Talking about your place of residence

CHECK   **Find language in this unit which is another way to say:**

1 the opposite of *commercial* (when talking about a building or part of a building)
2 ten floors in total
3 My flat is on the ground floor, next to the lift.

CHALLENGE   **Write a short description of your place of residence in your first language. Include your feelings about it. Then translate it into English. Ideally, use an English–English dictionary.**

Grammar for talking about your personal circumstances

CHECK   **In this unit, find an example of:**

1 the present simple used to talk about personal circumstances.
2 the present continuous used to talk about personal circumstances.

CHALLENGE   **From memory, summarize the rule about when to use the present simple and when to use the present continuous when talking about personal circumstances.**

Collocations

CHECK   **Check or remember the prepositions needed to complete these phrases.**

1 I'm doing a degree .... Physics.
2 I'm currently working .... an office cleaner, but it's only temporary.

CHALLENGE   **Complete these phrases with alternative examples to the ones given in the unit.**

1 work **in** .... *(a trade/profession, e.g. advertising)*
2 work **for** .... *(a company/organization)*
3 working **on** .... *(an example of a project)*
4 live **in** .... *(part of a building)*
5 live **on** .... *(part of a building)*

Pronunciation

CHECK   **Look at this sentence. Underline the words which would typically be stressed when saying them.**

I live with my parents in a flat on the top floor of a 15-storey building, not far from the city centre.

Now put lines under the words which could typically be run together in connected speech.

CHALLENGE   **Repeat the task above with sentences from websites or printed material. Blogs can be a good source of informal English about experiences and opinions.**

UNIT 2 ▶ Leisure interests

SPEAKING PART 1: FREE-TIME ACTIVITIES

In Part 1 of the Speaking test, the examiner may ask questions about your free-time activities and entertainment interests. Questions of this type may begin the interview, or they may follow on from other questions, for example questions about your occupation or the place where you live. It's a good idea to prepare some ideas for speaking about these things and the other typical Part 1 topics which you will meet later in this book.

Try it first!

Try talking about your leisure interests as if you were doing Speaking Part 1. If you are working with a partner, take it in turns to play the roles of examiner and candidate. Here are some typical questions.

Examiner (*perhaps following on from questions on another topic*): Let's talk about your free-time activities.

● What do you do at the weekends?
● What is it that you like about [*one of candidate's leisure activities*]?
● How often do you get the chance to [*one of candidate's leisure activities*]?
● How important a part of your week are your free-time activities?
● Do you enjoy your free time more now than you did when you were a child?
● What free-time activity would you like to try in the future?

Spotlight 1

Useful language for talking about your leisure interests

Grammar: gerunds and infinitives

Gerund

The gerund ends in *–ing*.

I love **reading**.

I'm not very interested in **watching** *sport on TV*.

For activities, the gerund can often follow *go*.

I often **go swimming** *at the weekends*.

I'm **going fishing** *next weekend*.

Infinitive

The infinitive is the form of the verb found in the dictionary, and is often preceded by *to*.

I don't get much time **to listen** *to music*.

I hope **to have** *more free time from next year*.

I'm planning **to take** *my children to the zoo next Saturday*.

1 Put each of these gerunds and phrases with gerunds into the correct column of the table below.

camping   gardening   ice skating   mountain climbing
playing computer games   playing football   reading   running
skiing   walking in the countryside   walking the dog   watching TV

Tip
Make sure you learn the words in English for all your free-time and leisure interests. Write them in your vocabulary notebook, and use a dictionary or internet search to find out which ones can follow go.

can follow *go*	do not normally follow *go*

2 Choose the correct form (gerund or infinitive) in these sentences.

1 I always enjoy *to see / seeing* my friends.
2 I'm going *to see / seeing* it in the cinema as soon as it comes out.
3 We try *to go / going* to the theatre at least once a year.
4 We had a great time *to play / playing* silly games on the beach.
5 I'm planning *to buy / buying* some roller skates.
6 I'd like *to have / having* more free time, but it's impossible at the moment.

Both forms are possible with *like, love* and *prefer*. The second is more commonly used in American English.

I **like going** *to restaurants*. / *I* **like to go** *to restaurants*.

I don't really **like going** *shopping*. / *I don't really* **like to go** *shopping*.

We **love cooking**. / *We* **love to cook**.

Do you **prefer watching** *sport live or on TV?* / *Do you* **prefer to watch** *sport live or on TV?*

Tip
If you're not sure if a phrase is grammatically correct, enter it into an internet search engine. You'll probably see from the search results whether or not your version is correct. This also works for spelling, of course.

3 Write two sentences about your free-time activities using a gerund form.

4 Write two sentences about your free-time activities using an infinitive form.

Grammar: *used to*

> The examiner may ask you to compare your free time now with your free time in the past. In this case, *used to* can be very useful.
>
> I **used to** *play football every weekend, but I haven't done it for a long time now.*
> I **used to** *go running about once a week.*
> I **used to** *have a lot more free time than I do now.*
>
> Note the negative and question forms (although these are less likely to be useful in the Speaking test).
>
> I **didn't use to** *go swimming very often.*
> **Did you use to** *go swimming more often than you do now?*

5 Complete these sentences with your own ideas.

1 I used to .... , but now I don't.

2 I used to .... less often than I do now.

3 I used to .... more often than I do now.

Vocabulary: adjectives to describe leisure activities

6 Match the words/phrases on the left (1–7) with the words/phrases on the right (a–g) which mean the same thing.

1 relaxing	**a** affordable
2 exciting	**b** dull
3 fun	**c** enjoyable
4 boring	**d** family-friendly
5 expensive	**e** good for winding down
6 cheap	**f** high-cost
7 suitable for children	**g** stimulating

> **Tip**
> It can be a good idea to try to use less-common words and phrases. This shows you have a large vocabulary.

Vocabulary: collocations and expressions connected with leisure activities

7 These expressions can be useful when describing a leisure activity. Use them to complete the sentences below.

go for a	have fun	have some time off from	let my hair down
relax with	sit back	taking it easy	unwind

1 I quite often .... drink after work with some of my colleagues.

2 It's very important to .... together as a family.

3 After a hard day, sometimes it's nice just to .... and watch some rubbish on TV.

4 I find it a really good way to .... the pressures of work and raising a family.

5 People tell me I should try to .... sometimes. I find it really difficult to relax.

6 My idea of a good time is to turn off my phone and .... a good book for a couple of hours.

7 I plan to spend next weekend ....

8 I really like to .... by having a nice, hot bath. It helps me relax after a hard day in the office.

Exam skills 1

Giving plenty of detail in descriptions

As you saw in Unit 1, it's a good idea to give plenty of detail in descriptions. For example, don't just say *I like sport* or *I read a lot*. Give more details:

● *I'm very keen on sport and keeping fit in general. I play football for my college team and I go to the gym two or three times a week.*
● *I read a lot and I often have two or three books on the go at the same time. At the moment, I'm reading a collection of Sherlock Holmes short stories and also a book about the history of China.*

1 Write a suitable description of one of your main leisure interests.

Tip
If you have several free-time interests, choose the one which will be most interesting to speak about, and will demonstrate your ability to use a wide range of English structures and vocabulary.

Adding reasons

It's often a good strategy to give reasons for your answers, and sometimes the examiner's question may specifically ask for a reason. In these examples, the candidate explains how a leisure activity improves his/her life.

● *My work is quite stressful, so at the weekends I like to take it really easy.*
● *I like it because it's a very sociable activity. I've made lots of new friends from doing it.*
● *I've always enjoyed being creative and I love music. Also, playing songs you've written to an audience is incredibly satisfying, even if it's only a small audience.*

2 Write a reason why the leisure activity you described in Exercise 1 improves your life.

Language check

3 Look at your answers to Exercises 1 and 2. Have you used gerund and infinitive forms correctly? Can you change the vocabulary to include some more advanced words and phrases?

Prepare and practise

4 Prepare your ideas for speaking about your leisure interests. Write some brief notes on ways to answer these questions. Can you use Spotlight 1 on pages 22–23 and the information above?

1 What do you do at the weekends?
2 What is it that you like about [*one of candidate's leisure activities*]?
3 How often do you get the chance to [*one of candidate's leisure activities*]?
4 How important a part of your week are your free-time activities?
5 Do you enjoy your free time more now than you did when you were a child?
6 What free-time activity would you like to try in the future?

Tip
Remember that you won't be able to write notes in Part 1 in the test, but doing it now will help you to organise your ideas.

5 If you are working with a partner, role-play talking about your free-time activities as if in Part 1 of the Speaking test – one person is the examiner and the other is the candidate. Use the same sample questions, and refer to the notes you made in Exercise 4 if you wish to. When you have finished, reverse roles and repeat.

Listen 1

1 🎧 **3** **Listen to the recording, which is based on Speaking Part 1. For each question, choose the correct letter: A, B or C.**

1 How much free time does the candidate have at the moment?
   A quite a lot
   B not very much
   C almost none

2 Where does the candidate do his hobby?
   A on a beach
   B on the sea
   C on any type of flat land

3 Why does the candidate think it's an exciting sport?
   A It's very interesting preparing the equipment.
   B The vehicles move very fast.
   C It can be dangerous.

4 When does the candidate do this sport?
   A all year round
   B about half the year
   C only in the middle of summer

5 Why does the candidate say he enjoys his free time more now than when he was a child?
   A He didn't have any interesting hobbies when he was a child.
   B He didn't have much free time when he was a child.
   C He used to find his hobby frightening.

2 Now look at the audio transcript on page 105 and check your answers.

3 Was the recording very different from your role-play (Exercise 5, page 24)? How was it different? How could you improve further?

Pronunciation focus: sentence stress and connected speech

4 🎧 **3** **In Unit 1, you worked to improve your use of sentence stress and connected speech. Listen to the recording again while reading the audio transcript on page 105. After each sentence, pause and repeat what you've just heard. Try to copy the sentence stress and connected speech.**

5 Work in pairs, asking each other the questions below. Again, one person is the examiner, the other is the candidate. When you have finished, reverse roles and repeat. Try to include improvements you noticed when you listened to the recording, and try to improve your use of sentence stress and connected speech.

● How important are hobbies and other free-time activities to you?
● When do you usually do your free-time activities?
● Do you share your free-time interests with friends?
● Do you have enough time for your free-time activities?
● What is the balance of work/study and free time in your life?

Tip
Do this regularly using the recordings that accompany this book. And of course, you can also do this with many other types of recording.

SPEAKING PART 1: MUSIC, FILMS AND BOOKS

Other common topics in the first part of the Speaking test are entertainment interests such as music, films, books, etc. Questions on these topics may follow on from more general questions about leisure activities and how they fit into your life, as shown in the first part of this unit.

Try it first!

Try talking about your music interests as if you were doing Speaking Part 1. If you are working with a partner, take it in turns to play the roles of examiner and candidate. Here are some typical questions.

Examiner (*perhaps following on from more general questions about free time*): Let's talk about music.

- What kind of music do you like listening to?
- Do you like listening to any other types of music?
- When do you usually listen to music?
- Has the kind of music you like changed over the years?
- Do you prefer listening to live music or recorded music?

Spotlight 2

Useful language for talking about music, films, books, etc.

Vocabulary: types of music, film and book

1 Put these types of music, film and book into the correct columns of the table below. The words in bold can go in more than one column.

action	classical	comedy	dance
detective	documentary	**horror**	humorous
independent	jazz	literary	low-budget
non-fiction	pop	reference	reggae
rock	**science fiction**	**thriller**	urban
western	biography/autobiography		

music	film	book

Tip
Learn the specific words in English for all the types of music, film and book you like.

2 These words are based on words to describe films in Exercise 1. What kind of film do you think they describe? Can you think of an example for each?

1 sci-fi   2 rockumentary   3 biopic   4 rom-com   5 no-budget

Vocabulary: likes and dislikes

3 How much does the speaker like it? For each sentence, choose a number on a scale of 1 to 5 (1 = likes very much, 3 = neutral, 5 = doesn't like at all).

1 I quite like horror fiction.
2 I adore reading crime novels.
3 I'm not bothered either way about classical music.
4 Most rock music leaves me cold.
5 I'm obsessed with early-eighties electronic music.
6 I can't stand opera and ballet.
7 I'm not very keen on low-budget films.
8 I can't get enough science fiction.
9 I don't really have an opinion about jazz.
10 I'm a big fan of independent, low-budget cinema.

4 Complete the sentences from Exercise 3 with your own ideas relating to this theme.

1 I quite like ....
2 I adore ....
3 I'm not bothered either way about ....
4 .... leaves me cold.
5 I'm obsessed with ....
6 I can't stand ....
7 I'm not very keen on ....
8 I can't get enough ....
9 I don't really have an opinion about ....
10 I'm a big fan of ....

Exam skills 2

Avoiding being too general

> General statements such as *Music is very important to me* are OK for beginning a reply, but they don't demonstrate your ability to use English for complex purposes.

1 Give each of these replies a grade from 1 to 5 depending on how well you think it demonstrates the candidate's ability (5 is the highest).

1 My tastes have changed over the years. I used to listen to a lot of very commercial pop music. Now I mostly listen to rock and jazz.

2 I love music. I listen to it nearly every day, and I can't imagine living without it. It's one of the most important things in my life.

3 Music used to play an important role in my life. I used to talk about the latest releases for hours with my friends. These days, though, I'm much less interested in it.

4 There's so much music out there, it can be difficult to know where to start. Doubtless there are amazing bands I'd love if I discovered them, but I don't really have time to track them down.

5 I listen to many different kinds of music. My favourite is rock, but I also listen to pop and rap. Sometimes I also listen to classical and jazz, but not very often. I don't have any classical or jazz CDs, but I have some albums on my computer.

Asking for repetition

2 Complete these ways of asking the examiner to repeat the question using *catch*, *repeat* and *say*.

1 Could you .... that again, please?

2 Sorry, I didn't .... that.

3 Sorry, could you .... the question?

Tip
If you're not sure that you understood the question correctly, ask the examiner to repeat it. You won't normally lose marks for doing this – after all, it happens in native-speaker conversations, too.

Prepare and practise

3 On a separate piece of paper, write answers to each of these questions which include plenty of detail and avoid being too general.

1 What kinds of film and TV do you like watching?

2 Do you like watching any other types of film and TV?

3 When do you usually watch films?

4 Have the types of film and TV programme you like changed over the years?

5 Do you prefer watching films on TV or in the cinema?

6 What kinds of book and magazine do you like reading?

7 Do you like reading any other types of book?

8 When do you usually read?

9 Have the types of book you like changed over the years?

10 Do you prefer reading books or newspapers and magazines?

Tip
The examiner may ask you to discuss one topic for the first half of the Part 1 test, then switch to another topic for the second half. This is normal, and doesn't mean that your performance for the first topic was inadequate.

4 Work in pairs. One person is the examiner, the other is the candidate. The examiner asks questions 1–5 from Exercise 3. Then reverse roles and repeat with questions 6–10. Refer to the answers you wrote.

5 Repeat, but reverse roles, so that the person who asked questions 1–5 the first time now answers them, and vice versa. This time, don't refer to the answers you wrote – try to include all the information from memory.

Listen 2

1 🎧 **4** **Listen to the recording, which is based on Speaking Part 1. For each question, choose the correct letter: A, B or C.**

1 The candidate
  A loves magazines.
  B hates magazines.
  C is not interested in magazines.

2 The books which most interest the candidate are
  A novels.
  B novels and reference books.
  C biographies and reference books.

3 The candidate
  A quite likes crime fiction.
  B loves crime fiction.
  C likes novels set in Italy.

4 The candidate's tastes in reading have
  A changed a lot recently.
  B changed a little since becoming an adult.
  C not changed since becoming an adult.

5 The candidate spends
  A about the same amount of time reading novels and newspapers.
  B more time reading newspapers than novels.
  C more time reading novels than newspapers.

2 **Now look at the audio transcript on page 106 and check your answers.**

3 **Was the recording very different from your role-play (Exercises 4 and 5, page 28)? How was it different? How could you improve further?**

Pronunciation focus: whole sentence intonation

4 a 🎧 **4** **Listen to the recording again. Notice the intonation of whole sentences. How is intonation used to divide the parts? Where are the falling intonations placed?**

b **Read the audio transcript on page 106 while you listen. Pause the recording after each sentence and copy the intonation of the speaker.**

5 **Work in pairs, asking each other the questions below. Again, one person is the examiner, the other is the candidate. When you have finished, reverse roles and repeat. Try to include improvements you noticed when you listened to the recording, and try to improve your whole sentence intonation.**

  ● Do you enjoy watching sport on TV?
  ● Do you like advertisements on TV?
  ● How important is radio in your life?
  ● How much of your entertainment is based on the Internet?
  ● Do you ever watch films or TV programmes in a foreign language?

Check and challenge

Talking about leisure interests and activities

CHECK **Based on this unit, find three alternative ways to say each of the following:**

1 I like it
2 I don't like it
3 take it easy
4 low-cost

CHALLENGE **In your first language, write a short description of a leisure activity you enjoy. Include your feelings about it. Then translate it into English. Ideally, use an English–English dictionary.**

Talking about things you watch and read

CHECK **What genre(s) does each of these titles suggest? (All the genres are included in this unit.)**

1 *Dawn of the Vampires*
2 *Inspector May's Last Case*
3 *The Baubles: Greatest Hits Volume II*
4 *Andy Warhol: Life as Art*

CHALLENGE **1 Make a list or your five favourite genres, starting with your most favourite.**

2 In your first language, write the reasons why you like your favourite genre. What are the things about it you enjoy? Then translate what you've written into English. Ideally, use an English–English dictionary.

Grammar for talking about leisure interests and activities

CHECK **In this unit, find a grammatical form:**

1 which converts a verb to a word which can be used in the same way as a noun.
2 for talking about regular habits in the past, especially discontinued ones.
3 for giving reasons.

CHALLENGE **How many gerunds can you think of which could fill the gap in this sentence?**
I went .... last weekend.

Pronunciation

CHECK **Look at these sentences. In each one, underline the words which would typically be said with a slight falling intonation to divide the ideas.**

1 I quite like horror films, but not if they're excessively violent.
2 I read less than I used to because I don't have very much free time at the moment.
3 I'd rather watch a film in the comfort of my own home than travel to a cinema, stand in a queue to buy tickets and then have to sit next to lots of noisy kids eating popcorn.

CHALLENGE **Repeat the task above with sentences from websites or printed material. Blogs can be a good source of informal English about experiences and opinions.**

UNIT 3 | # Finding your own path

SPEAKING PART 1: YOUR OCCUPATION

In Part 1 of the Speaking test, the examiner asks you questions on familiar topics about your personal life and interests. Note that this is not usually related to the topics that follow in Parts 2 and 3.

Try it first!

1 **Here are some typical Part 1 questions relating to occupations. Make notes on your ideas for answering them. Include details, opinions and reasons as you saw in Units 1 and 2. (You won't be able to make notes in the exam, but it can help you to organize your ideas now.)**

- Do you enjoy your occupation?
- What's the most difficult part of your occupation?
- Do you think your occupation is stressful? (Why? / Why not?)
- What's the best part of your day when you are working/studying?
- What changes would improve your typical day?

2 **Work in pairs. One person plays the role of the examiner, the other plays the role of the candidate. Ask and answer the questions from Exercise 1. The candidate refers to the notes he/she made. When you have finished, reverse roles and repeat.**

3 **Repeat the process with these questions. This time, do it without making notes first.**

- Have you ever had an interview for a job or to become a student?
- Do you like interviews? (Why? / Why not?)
- Is it easy to find a job where you live? (Why? / Why not?)
- What problems do people who can't find a job face?
- Why do some people dislike their jobs?

From this point in the book onwards, the main focus of the Speaking units is on Parts 2 and 3, as they tend to be more challenging. But of course, the language and skills you will learn are also useful for Part 1.

SPEAKING PART 2: YOUR JOB
(OR THE JOB YOU HOPE TO HAVE)

> In Part 2 of the Speaking test, the examiner gives you a task card like the one below. You then have a minute to prepare to speak for one to two minutes. You are allowed to make notes if you wish.

Try it first!

Before you study this section, try following the instructions on the card as if in Speaking Part 2. Work in pairs, taking it in turns to play the roles of examiner and candidate. This is what the examiner may say:

Examiner: You have one to two minutes for this. Don't worry if I stop you. I'll tell you when the time is up. Can you start speaking now, please?

> Describe the job or career you have or hope to have in the future.
> You should say:
>   what the job is
>   what the job involves
>   why you chose this job
> and explain what you like and/or dislike about this job.

Spotlight 1
Useful language for talking about occupations and career plans

Grammar: talking about the future

Tip
To get a high score, it's important to choose the correct grammatical forms when talking about the future. A common mistake is to use will for all future sentences.

1 **If you are a student, you may need to talk about your future career plans. Match the example sentences (1–5) with the usages (a–e).**

1 **present simple:** *I graduate next summer.*

2 **with *will*:** *It won't be easy to begin with.*

3 **with *going to*:** *It's going to be hard to begin with.*

4 **with *going to*:** *I'm going to apply to companies in this country and abroad.*

5 **present continuous:** *I'm taking my final exams next month.*

a predictions with evidence

b predictions without evidence

c future plans

d future arrangements, especially social arrangements

e scheduled events

Grammar: conditional futures

> Compare these sentences:
> *It will be nice to use my English in my daily work.*
> *It would be nice to use my English in my daily work.*
>
> The first sentence discusses a job which the speaker is certain he/she will have in the future. The second discusses a job which the speaker is not certain he/she will have.

2 Complete these sentences with the appropriate form of *will* in each gap.

1 I .... really like to teach in a university, but I .... need at least a Master's degree for that.

2 I .... want to work with children. That .... suit me at all.

3 It .... be easy to get my ideal job, but I'm going to try.

4 Of course, there .... be hundreds of other people applying for the job. I probably .... even be called for an interview.

5 I think I .... make a good teacher, but I .... want to spend the next 30 years going into a school every day.

6 I'm sure I .... find a nice job soon.

Vocabulary: prepositions

3 Complete the phrases below using the prepositions in the box.

for	from	in	of	to	with

1 graduate .... university

2 graduate .... the summer

3 apply .... a job

4 apply .... a company

5 experienced .... computers

6 have experience .... working for a large organization

Vocabulary: expressions for talking about the future

4 Work in pairs. Decide how soon these events will happen (1 = very soon, 2 = quite soon, 3 = in the distant future or perhaps not at all).

1 Eventually, I hope to enrol for a course. ☐

2 I'll be getting my exam results any minute now. ☐

3 At some point in the not-too-distant future, I'm going to apply for a course. ☐

4 My exam results are due shortly. ☐

5 I'm just about to apply for a course. ☐

6 I should be getting my exam results before too much longer. ☐

7 I'll be applying for a course sooner rather than later. ☐

8 I'll be getting my exam results in due course. ☐

Exam skills 1

Contrasting opposite ideas

1 Continue the second sentence in each example with your own ideas. Note that each one begins with a useful word/expression for contrasting ideas.

   1 The hours are long and the pay is low. **However**, ...

   2 I'd have to do a lot of travelling, which I don't really like. **Apart from that**, ...

   3 There's not much job security in this type of work. **On the other hand**, ...

   4 I'm not brilliant with computers. **Even so**, ...

Sequencing ideas

2 Put the sections of this example of a Part 2 talk in the correct order, so they match the instructions on the card on page 32.

a ☐

That mostly involves visiting farms, of course, but it's not just treating sick animals. A lot of the work is about preventing disease and testing for disease. For example, cows can catch tuberculosis from wild animals, so every cow in the country has to be tested for it regularly.

b ☐

At the moment, I'm studying to be a vet, so of course that's what I hope to become when I graduate next summer. I'm almost certain I'm going to pass my final exams!

c ☐

The pay can be very good, especially if you set up your own practice rather than working for somebody else, and I think I'll have a lot of job satisfaction. On the other hand, it's hard work, you have to go out in all kinds of weather and it can be quite repetitive. Imagine vaccinating five hundred pigs, for example.

d ☐

Generally, there are two types of vet, ones who work mostly with pets and ones who work mostly with farm animals. I wouldn't want to spend all day dealing with cats and dogs, so I'd like to be the second kind.

e ☐

Some people think I want to become a vet because I love animals, but that's not really the reason. I do like animals, but the real reason is that I want to work outdoors in the real world of agriculture. I wouldn't be happy getting up every day to go and sit in an office.

Giving examples

3 Find these strategies in the talk in Exercise 2 and underline them.

1 Comparing what most people wrongly imagine with the truth.
2 Giving a specific example to illustrate a general point.
3 Making a point by giving an example of something which is *not* going to happen.

Prepare and practise

4 The first stage of preparation is deciding what points to include in your talk. Which four of these do you think are the best topics to include?

1 a story about something amusing that happened at work
2 an explanation of why you haven't yet decided about your future career
3 the main duties of the job
4 the reason the job is suitable for your type of personality
5 descriptions of jobs you've had in the past
6 the advantages and disadvantages of the job
7 your feelings about the job
8 your education and studies

5 Look at these notes for the talk about working as a vet (see Exercise 2). Make similar notes for your own talk. (You don't have to make notes in the exam, but doing it now can help you prepare.) Remember the model you have just read (Exercise 2). You will need enough notes to speak for a similar length of time, and with a similar amount of detail.

- studying to be a vet
- farm animals, not pets
- not just sick animals – also disease prevention and testing
- cows, TB from wild animals
- reason: not I love animals, I like working outdoors in agricultural environment
- good pay, job satisfaction, meeting people
- hard work, all weathers, repetitive, get up very early

6 If you are working with a partner, take it in t
notes you made in Exercise 5. Wh
any areas which could be

7 The examiner often finishe
questions. For example:

Is it easy to get a first job as a ..
How long do you think you'll b

How would you answer these
questions in pairs.

Tip
It's often a good idea to give examples to illustrate some of your points. This will make the points clearer, and will help you demonstrate a wider range of language.

Tip
It's important to follow the instructions closely. If you're a student and don't have a clear idea about your future career, perhaps imagine a suitable job and talk about that.

Tip
Avoid going back and correcting any minor mistakes you make. It's usually better to continue your talk.

Listen 1

1 🎧 **5** **Listen to a candidate talking about his job as a waiter. Which THREE of these sentences are true?**

1 The job is very simple.
2 He enjoys meeting the customers.
3 It was his ambition to become a waiter.
4 He doesn't earn much money.
5 He likes the people he works with.
6 He dislikes the hours.

2 Now look at the audio transcript on page 106 and check your answers.

3 Was the recording very different from your talk (Exercise 6, page 35)? How was it different? How could you improve further? Discuss your ideas with a partner or in small groups.

Pronunciation focus: review

4 🎧 **5** **Listen to the recording again while reading the audio transcript on page 106. After each sentence, pause the CD and repeat what you've just heard. Try to copy the sentence stress, connected speech and intonation.**

5 Role-play giving talks based on the first instruction card below. One person is the examiner, the other is the candidate. When you have finished, reverse roles and repeat with the second card. Try to include improvements you noticed when you listened to the recording, and try to improve your use of sentence stress, connected speech and intonation.

Examiner: You have one to two minutes for this. Don't worry if I stop you. I'll tell you when the time is up. Can you start speaking now, please?

> Describe a type of work or study you enjoy doing. You should say:
> what the type of work/study is
> where and when you do it
> who you do it with
> and explain why you think this type of work/study is enjoyable.

> Describe an important choice you had to make about your future studies or work. You should say:
> where and when you had to make this choice
> what you had to choose between
> whether you made the right choice
> and explain how you felt when you were making your decision.

SPEAKING PART 3: WORK–LIFE BALANCE AND SALARIES

In Part 3 of the Speaking test, the examiner asks further questions connected to the topic of Part 2. These questions explore more abstract ideas and issues.

Try it first!

1 Before you study this section, try developing the theme of the previous section into the more abstract area of work–life balance. Work in pairs. One person is the examiner, the other is the candidate. Here are some suggestions for questions from the examiner.

- Do you think that the balance between work and free time in your country is about right?
- What problems can be caused by too much work?
- What can people do if they feel they are expected to do too much work?
- Why do you think some people become workaholics?

2 Now reverse roles and discuss these questions about salaries.

- Why do some countries have a minimum wage?
- What are the advantages and disadvantages of a minimum wage?
- Some company directors earn many times more than the average person. Do you think this is right?
- Are the top footballers and pop musicians really worth the huge amounts of money they can earn?

Spotlight 2

Useful language for talking about work–life balance

Talking about frequency

1 Put these frequency expressions in the correct column of the table below, according to their meaning.

all the time   continually   every now and then   from time to time
hardly ever   infrequently   occasionally   once in a blue moon
once in a while   regularly   the whole time   very occasionally

very often	sometimes	not often	almost never

Tip
When talking about general topics, it's often necessary to say how often things happen. You can add colour to what you say by using a wider range of vocabulary to do this.

2 Rewrite this sentence with the words describing frequency in the correct position.

I have to work late at the office.

1 all the time
2 hardly ever
3 from time to time (*two positions possible*)
4 regularly (*two positions possible*)

Alternatives to *usually*

3 Choose the correct option to complete each sentence.

1 Companies *general / generally* interview a number of candidates for each job.
2 Workers *tend to / tend* know more about what's really happening in the company than the bosses.
3 *Generally speaking / Generally saying*, salaries are higher in the private sector than in the public sector.
4 *On the whole / In the hole*, salaries haven't risen much over the last couple of years.
5 In my country, company directors are *mostly / most* middle-aged men.

Exam skills 2

Relating things to your own experience

> Occasionally relating your answers to your own experience can be a useful strategy for Part 3, as it's a natural basis for conversation. On the other hand, you shouldn't refer to your own experience too much. The examiner will expect you mostly to talk about general issues.

> **Tip**
> Learn fixed expressions such as the ones in Exercise 1. Practise using them as much as possible, so they are more likely to come into your mind automatically in the exam. Using fixed expressions can make your English sound more 'natural' and can help you get a higher score.

1 Complete these sentences with your own ideas on the topic of work–life balance. Note that each begins with a useful fixed expression for talking about your personal experience.

1 In my experience, …
2 I don't have much experience of …
3 I've found that …
4 From what I've seen, …
5 My experience is that …

Prepare and practise

2 Student A is the person who asked the questions about work–life balance in *Try it first!* Exercise 1 on page 37.
Student B is the person who asked the questions about salaries in *Try it first!* Exercise 2 on page 37.

Student A: On a separate piece of paper, write a complex answer to each of the questions about work–life balance. Try to relate at least one answer to your personal experience. For example:
Obviously it depends on the company, but my experience is that employers regularly expect people to work longer than the agreed number of hours per week.

Student B: Do the same for the questions on salaries.

3 Repeat the two role-plays from the *Try it first!* section on page 37. For the questions on work–life balance, Student B asks the questions and Student A answers, based on his/her written answers (but from memory rather than just reading them aloud).

4 Reverse roles and repeat for the questions on salaries.

Listen 2

1 🎧 **6** **Listen to a Speaking Part 3 conversation about work–life balance. For each question, choose the correct letter: A, B or C.**

1 The candidate thinks that in his country, work–life balance is most of all a problem for people

A who work in shops.

B with government jobs.

C who work for themselves.

2 He thinks that spending too long at work is bad for a person's

A personal relationships.

B health.

C personal happiness.

3 He thinks it's difficult for people to complain about working too much because

A other workers may resent them.

B the boss may think badly of them.

C it can be difficult to get a chance to speak to the boss.

4 He thinks workaholics are motivated by

A money.

B status.

C an inability to stop thinking about work.

5 The candidate's friend works very long hours because he

A needs the money.

B wants his work to be as good as possible.

C can't sleep at night.

2 **Now look at the audio transcript on page 106 and check your answers.**

Pronunciation focus: vowel sounds

3 **You are probably aware of the English vowel sounds which are most difficult for speakers of your first language. Using a cassette recorder, computer or mobile phone, read aloud and record sentences from the audio transcripts. Listen to them and compare them with the versions on the CD. If necessary, repeat until your vowel sounds are close to the examples in the recording.**

4 **Take the roles of examiner and candidate and practise speaking for Part 3 again, based on these questions, which explore more issues related to jobs and employment.**

● Should employers encourage workers to think of new ways to improve the company? Why?

● Why are new ideas and new ways of working sometimes unpopular with workers?

● What are the advantages and disadvantages of continuing to work in the same way?

5 **Swap roles and repeat with these questions.**

● What kind of technology do most office workers need to use?

● How can technology make workers' lives more stressful?

● What are the advantages and disadvantages of using video conferencing for meetings rather than meeting in person?

Check and challenge

Grammar for talking about the future

CHECK **Complete the gaps with the correct form of *will*.**

1 The speaker is going to work abroad:

'It .... be nice to work abroad.'

2 The speaker is discussing the possibility of working abroad:

'It .... be nice to work abroad.'

3 The person being asked is considering looking for this type of job:

'........................... it be very difficult to get this type of job?'

4 The person being asked has decided to look for this type of job:

'........................... it be very difficult to get this type of job?'

CHALLENGE **Complete these sentences with ideas about your occupation and/or career plans. How many sentences can you write for each?**

1 It will be ...

2 It would be ...

Conditional futures

CHECK **Rewrite this sentence as a conditional sentence (using *would*).**

I want to get a job with a major TV production company, but I'll have to move to the capital city of my country.

CHALLENGE **Write a conditional sentence with *would* about your own career plans.**

Contrasting ideas

CHECK **Rearrange these words to make four different ways to contrast opposite ideas.**

Apart   Even   from   hand   However   On   other   so   that   the

CHALLENGE **Use the four ways to contrast ideas you found above to contrast opposite ideas about the benefits of going to university and the benefits of starting work after leaving school.**

Relating things to your own experience

CHECK **Complete these phrases.**

1 In my .... , ...

2 I don't .... experience of ...

3 I've .... that ...

4 From what I've .... , ...

CHALLENGE **Complete the sentences above on the topic of the difference in pay between people at the top and people at the bottom of the earnings scale.**

Equal opportunities?

SPEAKING PART 1: YOUR EDUCATION

In Part 1 of the Speaking test, the examiner asks you questions on familiar topics about your personal life and interests. Note that this is not usually related to the topics that follow in Parts 2 and 3.

Try it first!

1 **Here are some typical Part 1 questions relating to education. Make notes of your ideas for answering them, including details, opinions and reasons. (You won't be able to make notes in the exam, but it can help you to organize your ideas now.)**

- Tell me about a school you went to when you were a child.
- Did you enjoy going to that school? (Why? / Why not?)
- Do you think it was a good school? (Why? / Why not?)
- Did you continue studying after you finished school?
- In what ways is higher education different to school?

2 **Work in pairs. One person plays the role of the examiner, the other plays the role of the candidate. Ask and answer the questions from Exercise 1. The candidate refers to the notes he/she made. When you have finished, reverse roles and repeat.**

3 **Repeat the process with these questions. This time, do it without making notes first.**

- Which school subjects did you enjoy most when you were at school?
- Were there any subjects you disliked?
- Did you enjoy doing homework? (Why? / Why not?)
- Why do you think schools usually give students homework?
- How did you feel about exams at school?

SPEAKING PART 2: SCHOOLS AND CHILDHOOD

> In Part 2 of the Speaking test, the examiner gives you a task card like the one below. You then have a minute to prepare to speak for one to two minutes. You are allowed to make notes if you wish.

Try it first!

Before you study this section, try following the instructions on the card below as if in Speaking Part 2. Work in pairs, taking it in turns to play the roles of examiner and candidate. This is what the examiner may say:

Examiner: You have one to two minutes for this. Don't worry if I stop you. I'll tell you when the time is up. Can you start speaking now, please?

> Describe a teacher who influenced you.
> You should say:
> >   when and where you met this teacher
> >   who the teacher was and the subject he/she taught
> >   why this teacher's lessons were special
> and explain how this teacher influenced you.

Spotlight 1

Useful language for talking about schools and education

Grammar: expressing obligation

1 When talking about school experiences, you may need to express degrees of obligation. Choose the most suitable option to complete each of these sentences.

1 At the school I went to, we didn't *have to / need to* wear uniforms.

2 I think all teachers *have to / should* think carefully about how much homework they set.

3 These days, most children *have to / must* study a broader range of subjects.

4 In my opinion, there *ought to / must* be more schools for exceptionally talented children.

5 I think that when I was growing up, there *should have / must have* been less emphasis on exams.

6 With some teachers, the pupils *had to / could* do whatever they wanted to.

7 I *don't need to / mustn't* explain the IELTS exam to you. You already know all about it.

Tip
To get a high score, it's important to choose the correct grammatical forms when talking about obligation. A common mistake is to use *must* when *have to* or *need to* would be the correct choice. Another common mistake is putting *to* after *must* and *should*. If you're not sure about these points, check the rules in a grammar book.

2 Match the phrases with the same meanings.

1 We couldn't do it.
2 We had to do it, although we didn't want to.
3 We didn't have to do it.
4 We shouldn't have done it.
5 We needed to do it.

a We ought not to have done it.
b It was necessary for us to do it.
c We weren't allowed to do it.
d We were forced to do it.
e We weren't required to do it.

Vocabulary: expressing obligation

3 Match the halves of these sentences relating to obligation.

1 There was no obligation to ...
2 It was up to us whether ...
3 It was our choice ...
4 In some lessons, we did more or less ...
5 We could pick and ...
6 We could ...

a choose what we did in lessons.
b as we pleased.
c do the homework in any one way.
d do what we liked at lunchtimes.
e how we did it.
f we did it or not.

Education systems vary from country to country, and the words for the schools you went to may not have exact translations. You can choose the nearest British English* or American English equivalents.

schools for ages 5–11 in the UK, 6–11 in the USA	primary school (British) / elementary school (American)
schools for ages 11–16 in the UK, 11–14 in USA	secondary school (British) / junior high school (American)
schools for ages 16–18 in the UK, 14–18 in USA	sixth-form college (British) / high school (American)

Year or *grade?*
British English tends to use *year*, whereas the American system uses *grade*. For example, the school year for ages 15–16 is *Year 11* in British English and *tenth grade* in American English.

* Reflects the system used in England and Wales, but not Scotland.

Vocabulary: collocations for talking about education

4 For each pair of words in italics, decide which one is correct. Or are both correct?

1 I *left* / *finished* school when I was 16.
2 I didn't always *make* / *do* my homework.
3 I *took* / *did* a university entrance exam in my final year at school.
4 I often *got* / *took* an 'A' in maths classes.
5 I didn't *do* / *make* very well in history tests.
6 At my school, we *had* / *did* PE* lessons every afternoon.
7 The teachers *set* / *gave* far too much homework.
8 Some teachers weren't very good at *keeping* / *making* discipline.

* physical education

Exam skills 1

Giving two or more points or examples

1 It may be useful to give two related points together to support your argument. Match the first points (1–4) with the second points (a–d).

1 Firstly, it's a good idea to give examples in your talk.

2 It's a good idea to give examples in your talk.

3 One thing to remember is that it's a good idea to give examples in your talk.

4 Two important points to remember are (a) it's a good idea to give examples in your talk and ...

a (b) it's a good idea to tell the listener when you are giving more than one example.

b Another is that it's a good idea to tell the listener when you are giving more than one example.

c It's also a good idea to tell the listener when you are giving more than one example.

d Secondly, it's a good idea to tell the listener when you are giving more than one example.

Tip
Using the organizing language in this section can help to demonstrate your ability to use spoken English for purposes such as explaining a complex situation or negotiating.

2 How could you adapt the language in Exercise 1 to give *three* points or examples?

Sequencing ideas

3 Put the sections of this example of a Part 2 talk about a former teacher in the correct order, so they match the instructions on the card on page 42.

a ☐ I've chosen her because she was obviously really enthusiastic about the subject. Most of the teachers I had were OK, but they gave the impression that it was just a job. Miss Zhang seemed really passionate about both history and teaching it.

b ☐ Another good thing about the lessons was that we didn't always have to study in a conventional way. For example, sometimes instead of writing an essay for homework, we were allowed to work with a friend to write an imaginary dialogue between two historical figures. Then if we wanted, we could perform it for the class, although there was no obligation to do that if we didn't want to.

c ☐ I'm going to talk about a history teacher I had at secondary school when I was about 15 years old. Her name was Miss Zhang.

d ☐ Secondly, she showed me how a teacher can use the students' own creativity to help them learn. Instead of just being a kind of audience for her lessons, we were involved in deciding what happened in the lessons. If I ever have to teach anything, I'll try to copy her method.

e ☐ I think Miss Zhang influenced me in two important ways. Firstly, she made me genuinely interested in history. I still read books on history and watch TV programmes about it when I get the chance.

f ☐ One of the best things about her lessons was that she gave us some control over what we studied and how we studied it. For example, she used to divide the class into groups, and each group could pick and choose which parts of the topic to study in more detail. Then we compared what we'd found out with the other groups.

4 Read the talk in Exercise 3 again. Find and underline all the language for helping the listener understand that you are giving two examples.

Prepare and practise

5 The first stage of preparing for a task like this is deciding who to talk about. Which of these examples do you think would be most suitable, and why?

a A teacher from primary school. You don't remember her particularly well, but she taught you to read and write.

b A teacher from secondary school who taught you maths. You disliked him, you didn't learn much about maths, and you believe he was a bad teacher.

c A teacher from secondary school who taught you history. You learned a lot about history, and you are still very interested in the subject.

d A college lecturer you have now for your degree. You find his lectures very interesting, and you're learning a lot from him.

6 Look at these notes for the talk about Miss Zhang (see Exercise 3). Make similar notes for your own talk. (You don't have to make notes in the exam, but doing it now can help you prepare.) Remember the model you have just read. You will need enough notes to speak for a similar length of time, and with a similar amount of detail.

- When, where and teacher's name
- Why special – enthusiastic for subject and teaching it
- Why lessons were good:
  - Pupils sometimes chose what to study
  - Pupils allowed to create and act out dialogues
- How she influenced me:
  - Made me interested in history
  - Showed me a good way of teaching, using pupils' creativity

7 If you are working with a partner, take it in turns to give your talks. Refer to the notes you made in Exercise 6. When you listen to your partner, do you notice any areas which could be improved? After the talk, share your ideas about this.

8 The examiner often finishes this part by asking one or two 'rounding-off' questions. For example:

Do you think most of this teacher's pupils appreciated his/her lessons?

Would you like to meet this teacher again now?

How would you answer these questions? Role-play asking and answering these questions in pairs.

1 🎧 **7** Listen to a candidate talking about a teacher who influenced her and complete this summary. Write no more than TWO WORDS in each gap.

The teacher taught drama at the speaker's primary school. He didn't come to the school **1** .... The speaker was a **2** .... child. The drama lessons made her more **3** .... The drama teacher forced her to play the lead role in the school play, and afterwards she had many **4** .... At secondary school, she stopped acting, but she'd like to meet the drama teacher again to **5** ....

2 Now look at the audio transcript on page 107 and check your answers.

3 Was the recording very different from your talk (Exercise 7, page 45)? How was it different? How could you improve further? Discuss your ideas with a partner or in small groups.

Pronunciation focus: vowel sounds

4 🎧 **7** Listen to the recording again while reading the audio transcript on page 107. After each sentence, pause the CD and repeat what you've just heard. Pay particular attention to the vowel sounds, as you did at the end of Unit 3.

5 Role-play giving talks based on the first instruction card below. One person is the examiner, the other is the candidate. When you have finished, reverse roles and repeat with the second card. Try to include improvements you noticed when you listened to the recording, and try to improve your vowel sounds.

Examiner: You have one to two minutes for this. Don't worry if I stop you. I'll tell you when the time is up. Can you start speaking now, please?

> Describe a school or college where you were a student. You should say:
> what type of school/college it was
> where it was
> when you studied there
> and explain how you felt about it when you were a student there.

> Describe a game you enjoyed playing when you were at school. You should say:
> what the game was
> when and where you played it
> who you played it with
> and explain why you enjoyed playing this game.

SPEAKING PART 3: EDUCATION AND LIFE CHANCES, EXAMS, THE RESPONSIBILITIES OF SCHOOLS AND TEACHERS

In Part 3 of the Speaking test, the examiner asks further questions connected to the topic of Part 2. These questions explore more abstract ideas and issues.

Try it first!

1 **Before you study this section, try developing the theme of the previous section into the more abstract area of school and exams in general. Work in pairs. One person is the examiner, the other is the candidate. Here are some suggestions for questions from the examiner.**

- Do you think the schools in your country are equally good, or are some better than others?
- How can a person's education affect their future life?
- Do you think exams are a fair test of what a person has learned?
- Do you think there's too much emphasis on exams in your country?
- Do you think we really need exams?

2 **Now reverse roles and discuss these questions about children's behaviour and interests.**

- Do many schools in your country have problems with children behaving badly in lessons?
- Why do you think some children behave badly in lessons?
- In your country, do you think most pupils find the school subjects interesting?
- Have schools in your country changed since you were at school?
- Do you think children today are different from children when you were younger?

Spotlight 2

Contrasting and organizing ideas

Tip
In all of the Speaking test, but especially in Part 3, you may need to discuss both sides of an argument. The language in this section can help you do this.

1 **Here are two contrasting ideas relating to the theme of this unit.**

Few people believe examinations are a perfect way to measure ability.
Most state education systems use them.

Link the two ideas using these words.

1 but   2 However   3 On the other hand   4 Although   5 though

Check your answers on page 118.

Tip
Two useful phrases are *As I said, ...* (to repeat a point) and *vice versa* (to say that the reverse of a point is true).
As I said, I don't know much about schools today.
A good teacher can make a boring subject interesting, and *vice versa*.

2 **Imagine you are taking the Speaking test. Earlier, you told the examiner you went to school in three different countries, so you aren't an expert in one country's education system. The examiner asks you another question about national education systems. Repeat your earlier point using *As I said, ...***

Exam skills 2

Relating things to how much you know or don't know

1 Complete these sentences with your own ideas on the topic of schools and children in general. Note that they include useful expressions for talking about the limitations of your knowledge.

1 I don't know much about the .... of today.

2 I don't know if .... has/have changed much since I was at school.

3 I'm not an expert on ....

4 I know quite a lot about ....

'Filling in'

2 Match these 'filling-in' phrases (1–5) with typical reasons for using them (a–e).

1 I've never really thought about that.
2 Let me think.
3 Let me see.
4 That's a good question.
5 I'm not sure.

a Giving yourself time to remember something.
b The topic is complex, and there isn't a simple answer.
c The idea is new to you.
d You don't have a firm opinion on the subject.
e The topic is complex, and you need time to organise your thoughts.

Prepare and practise

3 Student A is the person who asked the questions about school and exams in *Try it first!* Exercise 1 on page 47.
Student B is the person who asked the questions about children's behaviour and interests in *Try it first!* Exercise 2 on page 47.

Student A: On a separate piece of paper, write a complex answer to each of the questions about school and exams. Try to use some of the language from Spotlight 2 on page 47 and from above. For example:
QUESTION: *How can a person's education affect their future life?*
ANSWER: *That's a good question. A good education can lead to a good career. However, plenty of people who had a poor-quality education have gone on to be very successful in one way or another.*

Student B: Do the same for the questions on children's behaviour and interests.

4 Repeat the two role-plays from the *Try it first!* section on page 47. For the questions on school and exams, Student B asks the questions and Student A answers, based on his/her written answers (but from memory rather than just reading them aloud).

5 Reverse roles and repeat for the questions on children's behaviour and interests.

OK. WHO THREW THAT?!

www.CartoonStock.com

Listen 2

1 🎧 **8** **Listen to a Speaking Part 3 conversation about schools and children in general. For each question, choose the correct letter: A, B or C.**

1 What does the candidate say about lessons when she was at school?
A Very few children behaved badly.
B Some children behaved badly.
C Almost all the children behaved badly.

2 According to the candidate, why do children behave badly in lessons?
A They don't respect the teacher.
B The lessons are not interesting.
C They don't respect the teacher *and* the lessons are not interesting.

3 What does the candidate think about school subjects in her country?
A They are not very interesting for the students.
B They are all quite interesting except for maths.
C It's the teacher's job to make them interesting.

4 What does the candidate say about schools today in comparison with when she was at school?
A There are probably more computers.
B Too many students have mobile phones.
C Most schools have banned mobile phones.

5 What does the candidate say about children today in comparison with children when she was young?
A They have hardly changed.
B They spend more time using computers and mobile phones.
C They know more about the world.

2 **Now look at the audio transcript on page 107 and check your answers.**

Pronunciation focus: consonant sounds

3 **You are probably aware of the English consonant sounds which are most difficult for speakers of your first language. Using a cassette recorder, computer or mobile phone, read aloud and record sentences from the audio transcripts. Listen to them and compare them with the versions on the CD. If necessary, repeat until your consonant sounds are close to the examples in the recording.**

4 **Take the roles of examiner and candidate and practise speaking for Part 3 again, based on these questions, which explore more issues related to education.**

- Should schools ask students to give their opinions about lessons and teachers?
- What would be the advantages and disadvantages of asking for students' opinions about their schools?
- Why do you think some students lose interest in school?

5 **Swap roles and repeat with these questions.**

- How important do you think it is for schools to offer sports as part of the curriculum?
- In some countries, sports have become less important in schools. Why do you think this is?
- What are the advantages and disadvantages of making sports an important part of the school day?

Check and challenge

Language for talking about obligation

CHECK From the unit, find at least *two* other ways to say each of these sentences.

1 It was compulsory.
2 It was optional.
3 It was forbidden.

CHALLENGE Write a short description of your school in your first language. Include information about what was and was not compulsory, and your feelings about those things. Then translate it into English. Ideally, use an English–English dictionary.

Relating things to your level of knowledge

CHECK From memory, complete these phrases from the unit.

1 I don't .... about ...
2 I don't .... if ...
3 I'm not .... on ...
4 I know quite ....

CHALLENGE Complete the sentences above on the topic of variations in the quality of education in different types of school.

Language for contrasting ideas

CHECK Correct the mistake in each of these statements.

1 I enjoyed my school days however, but I didn't like the homework or the exams.
2 I enjoyed my school days. On my other hand, I didn't like the homework or the exams.
3 I enjoyed my school days, I didn't like the homework or the exams, although.
4 I enjoyed my school days. I didn't though like the homework or the exams.

CHALLENGE Write sentences about your experience of school using each of these words/phrases.

1 but   2 However   3 On the other hand   4 although   5 though

Organizing language

CHECK In your own words, summarize the rules for when to use these phrases.

1 As I said, ...
2 vice versa

CHALLENGE Write an example sentence which demonstrates the use of each of the above phrases.

UNIT 5 ▸ Getting from A to B

SPEAKING PART 1: CITY LIFE, EVERYDAY JOURNEYS

In Part 1 of the Speaking test, the examiner asks you questions on familiar topics about your personal life and interests. Note that this is not usually related to the topics that follow in Parts 2 and 3.

Try it first!

1 **Here are some typical Part 1 questions relating to city life. Make notes of your ideas for answering them. Include details, opinions and reasons. (You won't be able to make notes in the exam, but it can help you to organize your ideas now.)**

   ● Do you live in a big city or another kind of place?
   ● Do you like living in a big city? (*or* Do you like visiting big cities?)
   ● What kind of things do you like doing in a city?
   ● Do you think it's important for cities to have parks and other green spaces? Why?
   ● What kind of problems can big cities have?

2 **Work in pairs. One person plays the role of the examiner, the other plays the role of the candidate. Ask and answer the questions from Exercise 1. The candidate refers to the notes he/she made. When you have finished, reverse roles and repeat.**

3 **Repeat the process with these questions. This time, do it without making notes first.**

   ● Tell me about your daily journey to work or where you study.
   ● Is the public transport where you live good?
   ● What traffic problems are there in your area?
   ● How do these traffic problems affect you?
   ● What would help improve the traffic situation in your area?

SPEAKING PART 2: TOWNS, CITIES AND URBAN TRANSPORT

In Part 2 of the Speaking test, the examiner gives you a task card like the one below. You then have a minute to prepare to speak for one to two minutes. You are allowed to make notes if you wish.

Try it first!

Before you study this section, try following the instructions on the card as if in Speaking Part 2. Work in pairs, taking it in turns to play the roles of examiner and candidate. This is what the examiner may say:

Examiner: You have one to two minutes for this. Don't worry if I stop you. I'll tell you when the time is up. Can you start speaking now, please?

> Describe a city you have visited. You should say:
> where the city is
> why you went there
> what you did there
> and explain how you felt about this city.

Spotlight 1
Useful language for talking about cities

General prepositions

above
at
by
for
in
of
on
with

1 Complete these sentences using the most suitable preposition from the box on the left. Use each preposition once only.

1 I had to go there .... a job interview.
2 I went .... train.
3 My friend lives in a second-floor flat .... a shop.
4 Most of the famous places are .... the city centre.
5 The streets were full .... shoppers.
6 There are quite a lot of homeless people there who live .... the streets.
7 My interview was .... a large university.
8 I didn't have a map or my phone .... me.

Prepositions of movement

2 Choose the most suitable preposition from each pair in italics.

1 The best way to get *around / over* Paris is on the Métro.
2 You have to drive *over / across* a big concrete flyover to get to the city centre.
3 Unfortunately, a big road goes *through / around* the middle of the park.
4 It takes at least an hour to get *over / across* the town centre by car at peak times.
5 You go *past / around* two or three shopping centres on the way to the airport.
6 You have to go *past / along* a short stretch of motorway to reach the airport.

Tip
Using the wrong preposition is a very common error. Always using the correct preposition can make a big difference to making your English sound more advanced.

Vocabulary: describing cities

3 Match the words and phrases on the left (1–10) with the ones on the right (a–j) to make phrases relating to towns and cities.

1	inner	**a**	congestion
2	urban	**b**	hour
3	rush	**c**	city
4	traffic	**d**	public transport system
5	state-of-the-art	**e**	monuments
6	pedestrian	**f**	regeneration
7	ring	**g**	going on
8	historic	**h**	precinct
9	a lot	**i**	of the city
10	outskirts	**j**	road

4 Complete this text using some of the phrases from Exercise 3.

I spent two weeks in Vienna last summer. My sister's married to an Austrian – they live there, and I was staying with them.

It seemed a great place to visit as a tourist. It's got a **1** .... , so it's really easy and cheap to get around, and there are lots of palaces, churches and other **2** .... , so there's plenty to see. I imagine you could stay for a month and still not see everything.

A lot of the historic centre is pedestrianized, and it's all really beautiful. I spent most of my time just wandering around while my sister and her husband were at work. The area north of the centre, where they live, used to have a lot of the typical problems associated with areas in the **3** .... – drugs, crime and very bad housing. But over the last few years, an **4** .... programme has completely transformed it, and there are now lots of fashionable restaurants, nice apartments, that kind of thing. Now it's very popular, and I get the impression it's really difficult to find a place to live. It was very hard for my sister and brother-in-law to find somewhere they liked.

The overall impression I have is that Vienna is a great place to visit, as I said, and it seems a good place to live if you're middle-aged and have plenty of money. But it's maybe not so good if you're young and poor. It seems very expensive, and in comparison with other capital cities I've seen, there doesn't appear to be **5** .... for young people.

Structuring

Ideally, your Part 2 talk should have a clear structure, with a beginning, a middle and an end. Avoid talking for too long in the beginning and middle parts so that you get the chance to make all your points before the examiner stops you. At home, practise preparing and delivering Part 2 talks with a clock in front of you. Aim for just under two minutes.

Part 2 talks should cover all the points on the card, but they don't necessarily have to divide the time equally between the points. In the example on page 53 (Exercise 4), the candidate covers the first and second points on the card quite quickly, and mostly speaks about the third and fourth points.

Tip
Giving your ideas in a logical order will help your talk to flow more smoothly, and will demonstrate your ability to organize and present ideas effectively.

1 The talk in Exercise 4 on page 53 has four sections, shown in writing as four paragraphs. Analyze the structure, and write the purpose of each section.

Section 1: *Name the place and explain reason for visit.*

Section 2: ....

Section 3: ....

Section 4: ....

Describing impressions

It's a good strategy to differentiate between facts and your personal impressions. Talking about your impressions can demonstrate your ability to use spoken English for complex purposes and can give you opportunities to use a wide range of language.

2 In Exercise 4 on page 53, find and underline all the language for helping the listener understand that you are giving your personal impression rather than a fact.

3 Choose the best option to complete each of these sentences.

1 It *seems / views* a sad city, in some ways.

2 The historic centre *looks / appears* to have been totally taken over by tourists.

3 It seemed to *me / my opinion* that the public transport system really needs improving.

4 I got the *view / impression* that there's always lots going on for people of all ages.

5 *I imagine / I'm imagining* that not many people live in the city centre.

6 *I've guessed / I'd guess* that most of the people you see working in the centre have commuted in from the suburbs.

7 The *overall / total* impression I *make / have* is that most of the people who live there don't go into the centre very often.

8 You get *feelings / the feeling* that it must be quite difficult to live there.

Tip
If you want to give more than one personal impression, it's a good idea not to use the same impression phrase every time.

4 Decide whether each of these sentences represents a fact (F) or an opinion (O).

1 It's the best city in the world.

2 It's the biggest city in the world.

3 I've calculated that there are ten different ways I could get to work each morning.

4 I reckon there must be ten different ways I could get to work each morning.

5 I believe a new bridge is going to be built soon.

6 I expect a new bridge is going to be built soon.

7 I suppose a new bridge is going to be built soon.

Prepare and practise

5 **The first stage of preparing for a task like this is deciding which city to talk about. Do you think each of these pieces of advice is good or bad?**

1 Choose a city you visited fairly recently, so it will be easy to remember things to talk about.
2 Make a mental list of every city you have visited, and choose the most suitable.
3 Avoid choosing a city you only visited briefly and didn't see much of.
4 It must be a big famous city. Don't choose a small city that few people have heard of.

6 **Which four of these topics do you think are the best to include?**

1 the location of the city
2 your reason for travelling to the city
3 your journey to the city
4 what happened to you when you were in the city
5 the history of the city
6 descriptions of people you met in the city
7 your impressions of the city
8 what happened on your return from the city

> **Tip**
> It's important to choose a subject you can talk about for up to two minutes without running out of ideas.

7 **Write your talk about a city you have visited. In the exam, of course, you can't write what you are going to say in full. However, doing it now can be a good way to prepare your ideas and to practise using new language. To be the correct length, it should be around 200–250 words.**

8 **If you are working with a partner, put your written examples out of sight and take it in turns to give your talks. When you listen, do you notice any areas which could be improved? After the talk, share your ideas about this.**

9 **The examiner often finishes this part by asking one or two 'rounding-off' questions. For example:**

Do you think you will visit this city again?
Would you like to live in this city?
Would you recommend other people to visit this city?
In general, do you like big cities?

How would you answer these questions? Role-play asking and answering these questions in pairs.

Listen 1

1 🎧 ⑨ **Listen to a candidate speaking about a city she has visited. Which TWO reasons does she give for choosing to speak about Lecce?**

A She hasn't visited many other places.

B It's very beautiful.

C It's very well known in Italy.

D She visited several times and remembers it well.

E It's an interesting place to talk about.

2 **What does the candidate say about Lecce? For each question (1–3), choose the correct opinion (A–F).**

A old-fashioned   D relaxed

B interesting   E beautiful

C unexpectedly pleasant   F ordinary

1 Most of the city is ....

2 The historic centre is ....

3 The shops are ....

3 **Now look at the audio transcript on page 108 and check your answers.**

> **Tip**
> If your personal experience doesn't match the task very well, perhaps include a short explanation of why you've chosen your subject.

4 **The candidate had two problems:**

1 She has never visited another major city.

2 She doesn't know many facts about Lecce.

How did she solve each one? Discuss your ideas in pairs. Check the audio transcript again if you wish.

Pronunciation focus: consonant sounds

5 🎧 ⑨ **Listen to the recording again while reading the audio transcript on page 108. After each sentence, pause the CD and repeat what you've just heard. Pay particular attention to the consonant sounds, as you did at the end of Unit 4.**

6 **Role-play giving talks based on the first instruction card below. One person is the examiner, the other is the candidate. When you have finished, reverse roles and repeat with the second card. Try to include improvements you noticed when you listened to the recording, and try to improve your consonant sounds.**

Examiner: You have one to two minutes for this. Don't worry if I stop you. I'll tell you when the time is up. Can you start speaking now, please?

> Describe a museum or art gallery you enjoyed
> visiting. You should say:
>   what and where this place is
>   when you visited it
>   who you visited it with
> and explain why you enjoyed visiting this place.

> Describe a shop you enjoy visiting. You should
> say:
>   what type of shop it is
>   where it is
>   when and why you go there
> and explain why you enjoy visiting it.

SPEAKING PART 3: URBAN DEVELOPMENT AND INFRASTRUCTURES, MIGRATION TO CITIES

In Part 3 of the Speaking test, the examiner asks further questions connected to the topic of Part 2. These questions explore more abstract ideas and issues.

Try it first!

1 **Before you study this section, try developing the theme of the previous section into the more abstract area of urban life in general. Work in pairs. One person is the examiner, the other is the candidate. Here are some suggestions for questions from the examiner.**

- Do you think life is better in the city or in the countryside?
- In many countries, cities are growing fast. Why do you think this is?
- What problems can rapidly expanding cities have?
- Some cities receive millions of tourists. What problems can this cause?
- What can be done to ensure tourism doesn't cause too many problems?

2 **Now reverse roles and discuss these questions.**

- What are the benefits of living in the suburbs rather than the city centre?
- What are the disadvantages of living in the suburbs rather than the city centre?
- What problems can commuters face?
- What makes a good public transport system in a city?
- What can be done to reduce the amount of traffic in cities?

Spotlight 2

Grammar: conditional sentences

When talking about the development of cities and many other IELTS topics, you may need to use conditional sentences to describe processes of cause and effect.

1 **Match the usage explanations (1–4) with the example sentences (a–d).**

1 The zero conditional is useful for talking about processes of cause and effect which occur regularly.

2 The first conditional can describe possible or probable processes of cause and effect in the future.

3 The second conditional is useful for suggesting alternative processes of cause and effect.

4 The third conditional can describe how things would have or could have been different.

a If this city keeps growing, eventually it will join up with the towns around it.

b It would have been better if the airport had been built further from the city.

c If cities grow too quickly, they become chaotic and unhealthy places to live.

d If the government spent more money on developing rural areas, people wouldn't be so keen to move to the cities.

2 Complete these sentences with the correct forms of *to be* and *will* (if needed).

1 **Zero conditional:** If there .... a lot of traffic congestion in a city, it .... bad for local businesses.

2 **First conditional:** If the new transport system .... well planned, there .... any traffic congestion.

3 **Second conditional:** If there .... a lot of traffic congestion in a city, it .... bad for local businesses.

4 **Third conditional:** If the new transport system .... well planned, there .... any traffic congestion.

Exam skills 2

Clarifying

<table>
<tr><td>

In other words

By that I mean

To put it another way

I'm not saying

</td></tr>
</table>

1 Complete these sentences using the phrases in the box on the left.

1 City life can be hard work. .... that just doing basic things like getting to work and going shopping can be time-consuming and stressful.

2 I don't really like big cities. .... I don't enjoy some things, like the cultural activity and the monuments, but I'm always glad to get on the train and get back to the countryside.

3 There's not a lot going on socially or culturally in the village where I live. .... / .... , it's boring!

Personally, …

> Beginning a sentence with *Personally, …* means you know that what you're saying is only your opinion or preference, and many people will disagree. In Track 10, you will hear the candidate say:
>
> *Personally, I wouldn't want to live outside a city, but I've lived in Rome all my life.*

Tip
Clarifying your meaning, as shown in this section, demonstrates that you are able to give clear, precise meanings. It can also make your English sound more advanced and natural. Native speakers use clarifying strategies regularly to ensure their listeners fully understand the points they want to make.

2 Complete these sentences with your own ideas.

1 Personally, I can't stand .... , but I know they're/it's very popular.

2 Personally, I prefer .... to .... , but I'm probably in the minority.

3 Listen for clarifying phrases and *Personally, …* in the recording in the next section.

Prepare and practise

4 Student A is the person who asked the questions in *Try it first!* Exercise 1 on page 57.
Student B is the person who asked the questions in *Try it first!* Exercise 2 on page 57.

Student A: On a separate piece of paper, write notes for a complex answer to each of the questions from Exercise 1. Try to use some of the language from this unit.

Student B: Do the same for the questions from Exercise 2.

5 Repeat the two role-plays from the *Try it first!* section on page 57. For the first set of questions, Student B asks the questions and Student A answers, based on his/her written notes (but from memory rather than just reading them aloud).

6 Reverse roles and repeat with the second set of questions.

Listen 2

1 🎧 **10** **Listen to a Speaking Part 3 conversation about urban development. For each question, choose the correct letter: A, B or C.**

1 According to the candidate, the main benefit of living in the city is that
   A it's more interesting.
   B there are more jobs.
   C it's more convenient.

2 In some countries, large numbers of people move to the city
   A to find jobs.
   B because it has become impossible to live in their villages.
   C looking for a better standard of living.

3 Cities which expand very rapidly can have problems with
   A overcrowding and lack of public transport.
   B high levels of unemployment.
   C inadequate infrastructure.

4 Cities with too many visitors may
   A lose their original character.
   B become too crowded.
   C suffer from traffic congestion.

5 Cities should try to get visitors to
   A visit all year round, not just in the summer.
   B visit the less well-known parts of the city.
   C leave their cars outside the city.

2 **Now look at the audio transcript on page 108 and check your answers.**

Pronunciation focus: delivery speed

3 **If you speak too quickly, it may be difficult for the examiner to understand what you're saying, and you may make more errors. If you speak too slowly, you will not have enough time to answer all the questions fully. Using a cassette recorder, computer or mobile phone, read aloud and record sentences from the audio transcripts. Listen to them and compare them with the versions on the CD. If necessary, repeat until you are speaking at a similar speed to the examples in the recording.**

4 **Take the roles of examiner and candidate and practise speaking for Part 3 again, based on these questions, which explore more issues related to towns and cities.**
   ● What causes richer people to start moving into poorer parts of cities?
   ● How can this change a neighbourhood?
   ● How do the original residents tend to feel about this?

5 **Swap roles and repeat with these questions.**
   ● Why do so many cities have very tall buildings – skyscrapers – in their centres?
   ● In some cities, large areas of old buildings are being demolished to make way for new buildings. What are the advantages of this?
   ● What are the disadvantages?

Check and challenge

Prepositions

CHECK **Explain the difference in meaning between these pairs of phrases.**

1 go on a bus / go by bus
2 go over the river / go along the river
3 He lives in a street. / He lives on the streets.

CHALLENGE **Write a short description of your daily journey to work or college, or any other journey you do regularly. Be sure to use the correct prepositions.**

Describing impressions

CHECK **Rewrite these sentences, making it clear that they are personal impressions, not facts.**

1 It's a city with a very bright future.
2 The traffic has got worse recently.
3 It's safe to walk around at night.

CHALLENGE **Write a short description of the village, town or city where you live. Use vocabulary from this unit to be specific about its characteristics, and include your impressions.**

Conditionals

CHECK **This sentence is an example of the zero conditional:**

If more roads are built, traffic increases to fill them.

Rewrite it in the:

1 first conditional
2 second conditional
3 third conditional.

How does changing the grammatical form change the meaning?

CHALLENGE **Write answers to these questions about your village, town or city.**

1 How do you think it will change in the future?
2 How would it change if cars were banned from the centre?

Clarifying language and *Personally, ...*

CHECK **Correct the mistakes in these sentences.**

1 In another word, it's a really good place to live.
2 By that I'm meaning I didn't particularly enjoy my visit.
3 To put it the other way, it's an interesting place, but it can be exhausting.
4 I'm saying not that I wouldn't want to visit it again some time, though.

CHALLENGE **Write three sentences about your village, town or city beginning with *Personally, ...* Remember that these should be opinions that not everyone will agree with.**

UNIT 6 ▸ Dumbed down?

SPEAKING PART 1: NEWS AND ENTERTAINMENT

In Part 1 of the Speaking test, the examiner asks you questions on familiar topics about your personal life and interests. Note that this is not usually related to the topics that follow in Parts 2 and 3.

Try it first!

1 Here are some typical Part 1 questions relating to entertainment. Make notes of your ideas for answering them. Include details, opinions and reasons. (You won't be able to make notes in the exam, but it can help you to organize your ideas now.)

- When and where do you watch TV?
- What kinds of TV programme do you like watching?
- What other types of entertainment do you enjoy?
- How important is entertainment in your life?
- Do you use the Internet for entertainment?

2 Work in pairs. One person plays the role of the examiner, the other plays the role of the candidate. Ask and answer the questions from Exercise 1. The candidate refers to the notes he/she made. When you have finished, reverse roles and repeat.

3 Repeat the process with these questions. This time, do it without making notes first.

- Do you buy newspapers, or do you get news from somewhere else?
- What kind of news stories most interest you? Why?
- What kind of news stories are you not interested in? Why not?
- How important is following the news to you?
- How has your interest in the news changed since you were younger?

SPEAKING PART 2: TELEVISION

In Part 2 of the Speaking test, the examiner gives you a task card like the one below. You then have a minute to prepare to speak for one to two minutes. You are allowed to make notes if you wish.

Try it first!

Before you study this section, try following the instructions on the card as if in Speaking Part 2. Work in pairs, taking it in turns to play the roles of examiner and candidate. This is what the examiner may say:

Examiner: You have one to two minutes for this. Don't worry if I stop you. I'll tell you when the time is up. Can you start speaking now, please?

> Describe a TV programme you enjoy watching.
> You should say:
>   what the programme is
>   what it is about
>   when you watch it
> and explain why you enjoy it.

Spotlight 1

Useful language for talking about television and other types of entertainment

Grammar: complex comparatives

1 Write sentences comparing two TV programmes you know about using these structures.

1 *a lot more* + adjective + *than*
2 *a bit less* + adjective + *than*
3 *even* + comparative adjective + *than*
4 *not quite as* + adjective + *as*

Grammar: complex superlatives

2 Write sentences about TV programmes using these structures.

1 *possibly the* + superlative adjective + *of all time*
2 *probably the least* + adjective + *ever*

Comparing things is a good opportunity to demonstrate the versatility of your English. Rather than saying *A is better than B*, qualify the comparison:
*A is **slightly** / **a little** / **significantly** / **considerably** / **very much** better than B.*

Inverting comparisons can also sound impressive:
B isn't quite as good as A.
B is considerably less interesting than A.

Vocabulary: genres

3 Match the types of TV programme (1–10) with the descriptions / typical subjects (a–j).

1	current-affairs programme	a	analysis of news stories
2	documentary	b	collection of short comic pieces
3	game show	c	comedy series usually set in a home or workplace
4	historical drama	d	contestants trying to win money
5	literary adaptation	e	cowboys and gunfights
6	sitcom	f	in-depth exploration of one non-fiction subject
7	sketch show	g	interviews with celebrities
8	soap opera	h	relationships and problems of a group of
9	chat show / talk show		characters
10	western	i	type of soap opera set in the past
		j	TV version of a well-known book

Vocabulary: talking about television

4 Complete the sentences below with the words in the box.

> cast   dubbed   episode   programme
> reality   season   series   subtitles

1 *Friends* was a sitcom which ran for ten ....
2 The very first .... is often called the 'pilot'. If viewers don't like the pilot, no more programmes will be made.
3 The programme has a large .... of memorable characters.
4 In Spain, most British and American programmes are .... into Spanish.
5 In Portugal, most British and American programmes are shown in the original language with Portuguese ....
6 The British English for *TV show* is *TV* ....
7 The American English for *series* is ....
8 A popular form of programme nowadays is .... TV, which is unscripted and features ordinary people rather than actors or presenters.

5 Complete these sentences. Use a dictionary if you need to.

1 The plural of *series* is ....
2 The popular British science-fiction programme *Dr Who* usually attracts around 6 million .... when episodes are shown for the first time.
3 Most American sitcoms have a laugh-track added afterwards, but many British sitcoms are recorded in front of a live studio ....
4 Now we have digital TV and about 50 different .... to choose from.
5 Terrestrial TV is broadcast from a transmitter and is received by an .... connected to the TV. Cable TV comes through a fibre-optic cable under the ground. .... TV comes from space and is received by a dish on the wall or roof of the building.

6 Complete these sentences with *see*, *watch*, *look* or *view*.

1 I .... about ten hours of TV a week.
2 Did you .... the first episode of the new series?
3 Some major football matches are on pay-per-............................. channels.
4 Yuck! Don't .... at the TV now. They're showing a really gory operation.

Exam skills 1

Choosing the best topic

1 Write down the titles of three TV programmes you like and what type of programme each one is. They should all be different types. Then evaluate them based on these questions.

- Do I know the grammar and vocabulary I will need to describe it?
- Is there enough to say about it to speak for up to two minutes?
- Can I think of anything interesting to say about it other than just describing it?

After considering these questions, choose one of your programmes.

Prepare and practise

2 **Complete these notes about your chosen TV programme.**

Type of programme: ....

Main features: ....

When you watch it: ....

Why you think it's good: ....

How it's broadcast (terrestrial, cable, satellite): ....

How long it's been running: ....

Whether it's popular: ....

How it compares to programmes of this type in general: ....

3 In the exam, of course, you can't write a full summary of what you are going to say. However, writing one can be a good way to prepare your ideas and to practise using new language. Write a full summary covering the information in Exercise 2. Include the important points from your notes and put them into a suitable order.

4 If you are working with a partner, put your written examples out of sight and take it in turns to give your talks. When you listen, do you notice any areas which could be improved? After the talk, share your ideas about this.

5 The examiner often finishes this part by asking one or two 'rounding-off' questions. For example:

How much TV do you watch?

Are there any types of TV programme you dislike?

How would you answer these questions? Role-play asking and answering these questions in pairs.

Listen 1

1 🎧 **11** Listen to a candidate speaking about a TV programme she enjoys and complete these notes. Use no more than THREE WORDS in each gap.

> ● Has been running for more than 20 years.
> ● Watches on regular terrestrial TV and **1** ....
> ● Prefers the version with **2** ....
> ● Sometimes **3** .... it and watches again.
> ● Thinks it's **4** .... than most sitcoms.
> ● Does not agree that it has become **5** ....

2 Now look at the audio transcript on page 109 and check your answers.

3 Was the recording very different from your talk (Exercise 4, page 64)? How was it different? How could you improve further? Discuss your ideas with a partner or in small groups.

4 Which of these things did the candidate do? What was the benefit of doing or not doing each thing? Discuss your ideas with a partner.

1 Described the format and the characters in detail.
2 Explained how watching the programme fits into her life.
3 Contrasted the programme with others in general terms.
4 Contrasted the programme with specific other programmes.
5 Contrasted a widely held opinion about the programme with her own.

Pronunciation focus: review

5 🎧 **11** Listen to the recording again while reading the audio transcript on page 109. After each sentence, pause the CD and repeat what you've just heard. Try to copy all aspects of the pronunciation and also the delivery speed, as you did in Unit 5.

6 Role-play giving talks based on the first instruction card below. One person is the examiner, the other is the candidate. When you have finished, reverse roles and repeat with the second card. Try to include improvements you noticed when you listened to the recording, and try to improve your use of sentence stress, connected speech and intonation.

Examiner: You have one to two minutes for this. Don't worry if I stop you. I'll tell you when the time is up. Can you start speaking now, please?

> Describe a film you enjoyed. You should say:
>   what the film was
>   where and when you saw it
>   what type of film it was
> and explain why you enjoyed it.

> Describe a song or other piece of music you like.
> You should say:
>   what the song or piece of music is
>   what kind of music it is
>   when and where you first heard it
> and explain why you like it.

SPEAKING PART 3: QUALITY OF AND RESPONSIBILITIES IN THE MEDIA

In Part 3 of the Speaking test, the examiner asks further questions connected to the topic of Part 2. These questions explore more abstract ideas and issues.

Try it first!

1 **Before you study this section, try developing the theme of the previous section into the more abstract area of media, entertainment and news in general. Work in pairs. One person is the examiner, the other is the candidate. Here are some suggestions for questions from the examiner.**

- Do you think the quality of TV in your country is generally good?
- What problems do you think can be caused by watching too much TV?
- What are the advantages and disadvantages of showing imported TV programmes?
- Do you think that the things children see on TV and in films can influence their behaviour?
- Do you think Hollywood films can change local cultures?

2 **Now reverse roles and discuss these questions.**

- How important do you think it is to keep up to date with news and current events?
- In your opinion, what is the best source of news: TV, newspapers, the Internet or something else?
- Documentary films for the cinema seldom attract large audiences. Why do you think this is?
- Some people feel there should be more serious documentaries and dramas on TV and in the cinema. Do you agree or disagree with this?
- What do you think could be done to promote more serious types of TV programme and cinema film?

Spotlight 2
Useful language for contrasting ideas

In Unit 4, you used some basic language for contrasting ideas. Here are two more advanced ways to contrast ideas.

1 In Track 12 (page 68), you will hear a candidate contrasting two ideas with *Having said that, ...* This can be useful for contrasting ideas which are contradictory.

I think it's very important to know what's happening in your country and in the world. **Having said that**, *I don't actually follow the news carefully every day.*

In this case, the candidate contrasts what she thinks with what she actually does. Note that the stress is on *said*.

2 You will also hear the candidate use *apart from (that)* ... to contrast an exception with a general rule.

They may be exciting for people who have a special interest in the subject, but **apart from that**, *they tend not to have a lot of appeal.*

I watch the news and some current-affairs programmes, but **apart from that**, *I watch very little TV.*

Apart from *checking the headlines on the Internet, I don't really follow the news.*

Tip
Good use of advanced, natural-sounding phrases for connecting and contrasting ideas is one of the things that can help get you a high score.

Complete these sentences with your own ideas on entertainment and the media.

1 I think watching films in the cinema is better than watching them on TV. Having said that, ...
2 I often find documentaries very interesting and feel I've learned a lot from them. Having said that, ...
3 I like .... , but apart from that, ...
4 Apart from .... , I don't ...

Exam skills 2

Amplification

1 Read the five model answers (1–5) and match them to these strategies (a–e).

a Give a hypothetical scenario of how things could be different.
b Refer to an ongoing debate.
c Start with an exception or exceptions, then describe the general rule.
d Expand the focus of the question, but make sure it still includes what the examiner asked.
e Start with an obvious idea, then add a less obvious, more philosophical idea.

1 *Do you think the quality of TV in your country is generally good?*
There are three or four channels which are quite high quality, and in particular we have an arts channel which produces some excellent programmes. But the majority of channels don't seem high quality to me. They show a lot of imported programmes, moronic game shows and repeats. There are far too many advertisements as well. On some channels, they take a half-hour programme and make it up to an hour with advertisements and trailers for other programmes.

2 *What problems do you think can be caused by watching too much TV?*
Obviously, it's not very good for the health to sit still for hours at a time. I know I always feel quite bad if I sit in front of the TV for an entire evening. In my opinion, there's also a danger that watching TV can become a substitute for real life. It's easier to sit at home and watch TV than to go out and meet people, but it's obviously better to go out and do something more social and active.

3 *What are the advantages and disadvantages of showing imported TV programmes?*
The advantage is that some imported programmes are very high quality. They're well written, well acted and cost a lot of money to produce. In that respect, they're often much better than anything produced locally. However, the disadvantage of showing a lot of imported programmes is that it means we haven't developed much of a TV production industry in my country. If we made more TV programmes, there would be more jobs for actors, directors, script writers, etc. and we might start making interesting programmes rather than mostly just silly game shows, as I mentioned before.

4 *Do you think that the things children see on TV and in films can influence their behaviour?*
This has been discussed a lot in the media, especially the question 'Does watching violence on TV make children violent?' In my opinion, children don't have a problem distinguishing between fantasy and reality. I wouldn't let my kids watch horror films, but that's because I think it would upset them, not because I think they'd start killing people! The area where I think TV and films really can change their behaviour is advertising. Children are very easy to influence. A lot of advertisements on TV are aimed directly at children, and some films these days seem little more than advertisements for toys or computer games.

5 *Do you think Hollywood films can change local cultures?*

Perhaps a combination of American films, TV and music can have an effect. A lot of young people dress in quite an American-looking style, and a lot of English words and phrases have entered our language. Some habits have changed, too. For example, young people drink more alcohol than their parents did. Perhaps that's because of influence from the media.

2 **Here's an example of amplification. A general statement is followed by a specific example.**

There are three or four channels which are quite high quality (*general statement*), and in particular we have an arts channel which produces some excellent programmes (*specific example*).

How many more examples of this can you find in the model answers in Exercise 1?

Giving complex, structured answers will gain you marks, but it may not always be possible. The model answers given above were written to demonstrate a range of strategies, and only the most advanced candidates can consistently give answers like these. Learn from these examples, but unless you need band 7.5 or higher, don't worry about giving such complex answers to every question yourself.

Prepare and practise

3 **Student A is the person who asked the questions in *Try it first!* Exercise 1 on page 66.**
   Student B is the person who asked the questions in *Try it first!* Exercise 2 on page 66.

   Student A: On a separate piece of paper, write notes for a complex answer to each of the questions from Exercise 1. Try to use some of the language from this unit.

   Student B: Do the same for the questions from Exercise 2.

4 **Repeat the two role-plays from the *Try it first!* section on page 66. For the first set of questions, Student B asks the questions and Student A answers, based on his/her written notes (but from memory rather than just reading them aloud).**

5 **Reverse roles and repeat with the second set of questions.**

Listen 2

1 🎧 **⑫ Listen to a Speaking Part 3 conversation about news reporting and the media in general. Answer these questions, based on what the candidate says.**

Questions 1–2
Complete these sentences with no more than TWO WORDS in each gap.

1 The candidate only follows the .... news stories.
2 She thinks newspapers are a better source of news than TV because there is more detail and ....

Questions 3–5

For each question, choose the correct letter: A, B or C.

3 She thinks documentaries are less popular than fictional films because
    A few good-quality documentary films are made.
    B most people prefer to be entertained than informed.
    C documentaries don't get shown in cinemas very much.

4 She thinks TV programme makers and film producers should be
    A required to make more serious programmes and films.
    B encouraged to make more serious programmes and films.
    C left to decide for themselves what they make.

5 She thinks film festivals
    A don't show enough documentaries.
    B mostly show documentaries and serious dramas.
    C help create an audience for independent films.

Pronunciation focus: the schwa

2 The 'schwa' sound (phonetic symbol /ə/) is very common in English, and not using it correctly is one of the commonest pronunciation mistakes for learners of English. Underline the schwa words in the sentences below. Remember to think about the whole sentence, not just the individual words. For example, said alone the vowel sound in *to* is /uː/, but in connected speech, it sometimes (but not always) becomes /ə/.

    1 I've often thought about moving to another internet provider.
    2 My brother works as a news reader for a local television channel.
    3 I'd love to be a famous actor earning millions of dollars per film.

3 Using a cassette recorder, computer or mobile phone, read aloud and record sentences from the audio transcripts. Listen to them and compare them with the versions on the CD. If necessary, repeat until you are using the schwa sound in a similar way to the examples in the recording.

4 Take the roles of examiner and candidate and practise speaking for Part 3 again, based on these questions, which explore more issues related to entertainment and the media.
    ● What are the advantages and disadvantages of sharing music, films and TV programmes over the Internet?
    ● Do you think the Internet should be more controlled by companies and governments? Why? / Why not?
    ● Do you think the Internet can provide all the entertainment most people need? Why? / Why not?

5 Swap roles and repeat with these questions.
    ● What benefits can watching television bring to children?
    ● Should parents limit the amount of time their children spend watching television? Why? / Why not?
    ● Do you think advertising directly to children should be banned? Why? / Why not?

Check and challenge

Genres

CHECK Write eight genres of TV programme from memory.

CHALLENGE Write a short essay about your TV viewing habits and preferences. Use vocabulary from this unit to be very specific about the types of programme you like.

Comparative and superlative statements

CHECK Put these sentences in order according to how much the speaker liked the TV programme (1 = the most, 6 = the least).

a It was better than some things I've seen.

b It was even better than I was expecting.

c It was one of the best things I've ever seen.

d It was possibly the least enjoyable programme I've seen so far this year.

e It wasn't as bad as I expected.

f It wasn't quite as bad as I expected.

CHALLENGE 1 Write a comparative sentence about TV with *even*.

2 Write a superlative sentence about TV with *ever*.

Language for contrasting ideas

CHECK Complete these statements with your own ideas on a theme related to TV or entertainment in general.

Apart from ...

Having said that, ...

CHALLENGE Create a special area in your notebook for language used to compare and contrast ideas. This type of language is especially useful for the IELTS Speaking test.

Pronunciation: the schwa sound

CHECK Excluding Exercise 2 on page 69, find six words in this unit which contain more than one schwa sound.

CHALLENGE 1 Underline all the schwa sounds on this page from the point of view of reading.

2 Now imagine somebody reading the page aloud, using natural connected speech. How many more sounds would probably become schwas?

UNIT 7 ▷ The world's your oyster

SPEAKING PART 1: HOLIDAYS AND TOURISM

> In Part 1 of the Speaking test, the examiner asks you questions on familiar topics about your personal life and interests. Note that this is not usually related to the topics that follow in Parts 2 and 3.

Try it first!

1 **Here are some typical Part 1 questions relating to holidays and tourism. Make notes of your ideas for answering them. Include details, opinions and reasons. (You won't be able to make notes in the exam, but it can help you to organize your ideas now.)**

- Describe a place you visited recently as a tourist.
- Did you have a good time there? Why? / Why not?
- Did you enjoy the journey there and back?
- What do you like doing on holiday?
- How important are holidays for you?

2 **Work in pairs. One person plays the role of the examiner, the other plays the role of the candidate. Ask and answer the questions from Exercise 1. The candidate refers to the notes he/she made. When you have finished, reverse roles and repeat.**

3 **Repeat the process with these questions. This time, do it without making notes first.**

- Which places in your country are popular with tourists, and why?
- Why do people enjoy visiting other places?
- What makes a good holiday, in your opinion?
- If you could visit any place for a holiday, where would you go?
- What do you dislike doing on holiday?

SPEAKING PART 2: HOLIDAY AND TRAVEL EXPERIENCES IN GENERAL

In Part 2 of the Speaking test, the examiner gives you a task card like the one below. You then have a minute to prepare to speak for one to two minutes. You are allowed to make notes if you wish.

Try it first!

Before you study this section, try following the instructions on the card as if in Speaking Part 2. (If you talked about a place you visited in Speaking Part 1 on page 71, choose a different place now.) Work in pairs, taking it in turns to play the roles of examiner and candidate. This is what the examiner may say:

Examiner: You have one to two minutes for this. Don't worry if I stop you. I'll tell you when the time is up. Can you start speaking now, please?

> Describe a place you visited on holiday. You should say:
> where the place is
> what type of place it is
> what you did there
> and explain why you enjoyed visiting it.

Spotlight 1

Useful language for talking about travel, tourism and visiting other places

Vocabulary: holidays and tourism

Complete the sentences below with the phrases in the box.

city break	gap year	high season	holiday resort
low season	out of season	package holiday	

1 A place which exists mainly for tourists and is often by the sea is called a
....

2 For beach holidays, the middle of summer is the .... Spring and autumn are the .... , and winter is ....

3 A three-night stay in Paris or New York is a ....

4 A deal which includes travel, accommodation and in some cases meals is called a
....

5 Some months spent travelling between finishing studies and starting work is called a ....

Tip
Non-defining relative clauses are a good way to insert extra information. Using them can make you sound more advanced and 'natural' than giving every piece of information in a separate sentence.

Exam skills 1

Choosing the best topic

1 Write down three places you have visited as a tourist and what type of place each one is. You can include visits to family members in other places and day trips. Unit 5 included talking about visits to cities, so if possible choose other types of place. Then evaluate them based on these questions.

- Do I know the grammar and vocabulary I will need to describe it?
- Is there enough to say about it to speak for up to two minutes?
- Can I think of anything interesting to say about it other than just describing it?

After considering these questions, choose one of your places.

Prepare and practise

2 **Complete these notes about your chosen place.**

Type of place: ....

What you did there: ....

Why you enjoyed being there: ....

How you travelled there: ....

Where you stayed: ....

At least two interesting features of the place: ....

At least two interesting adjectives to describe the place: ....

3 In the exam, of course, you can't write a full summary of what you are going to say. However, writing one can be a good way to prepare your ideas and to practise using new language. Write a full summary covering the information in Exercise 2. Include the important points from your notes and put them into a suitable order.

4 If you are working with a partner, put your written examples out of sight and take it in turns to give your talks. When you listen, do you notice any areas which could be improved? After the talk, share your ideas about this.

5 The examiner often finishes this part by asking one or two 'rounding-off' questions. For example:

Would you like to visit this place again?
What kind of visitor do you think this place suits best?

How would you answer these questions? Role-play asking and answering these questions in pairs.

Listen 1

1 🎧 ▶ **13** **Listen to a candidate speaking about a place he visited on holiday.**

Questions 1–2

Answer these questions using short answers. Use no more than TWO WORDS for each answer.

1 How did the family travel to Puertonuevo?

2 How was the beach at Puertonuevo?

Questions 3–5

Which THREE things did the candidate mention that he enjoyed?

A The beautiful town

B Eating in restaurants

C More freedom than at home

D Playing with other children

E Swimming in the sea

F The location of the campsite

G Games at the campsite

2 **Now look at the audio transcript on page 110 and check your answers.**

3 **Was the recording very different from your talk (Exercise 4, page 73)? How was it different? How could you improve further? Discuss your ideas with a partner or in small groups.**

Pronunciation focus: the schwa

4 🎧 ▶ **13** **Listen to the recording again while reading the audio transcript on page 110. After each sentence, pause the CD and repeat what you've just heard. Try to copy all aspects of the pronunciation and pay particular attention to the schwa sound, as you did in Unit 6.**

5 **Role-play giving talks based on the first instruction card below. One person is the examiner, the other is the candidate. When you have finished, reverse roles and repeat with the second card. Try to include improvements you noticed when you listened to the recording, and try to improve your use of sentence stress, connected speech and intonation.**

Examiner: You have one to two minutes for this. Don't worry if I stop you. I'll tell you when the time is up. Can you start speaking now, please?

> Describe a journey you enjoyed. You should say:
>   where you travelled
>   how you travelled there
>   how long the journey took
> and explain why you enjoyed it.

> Describe a national holiday which is important
> in your country. You should say:
>   when the holiday occurs
>   how you spent it last time
>   what you like and dislike about this holiday
> and explain why this holiday is important.

SPEAKING PART 3: RESPONSIBLE TOURISM

In Part 3 of the Speaking test, the examiner asks further questions connected to the topic of Part 2. These questions explore more abstract ideas and issues.

Try it first!

1 **Before you study this section, try developing the theme of the previous section into the more abstract area of travel and tourism in general. Work in pairs. One person is the examiner, the other is the candidate. Here are some suggestions for questions from the examiner.**

- Why do you think tourism is so popular and still increasing in popularity?
- Do you think people always get what they were hoping for on holiday?
- Why is tourism so important to some economies?
- What environmental problems can be caused by tourism?
- What can be done to reduce these environmental problems?

2 **Now reverse roles and discuss these questions.**

- Millions of Western tourists visit holiday resorts in developing countries. What do you think attracts them?
- What difficulties can Western visitors experience in developing countries?
- How can large numbers of Western visitors affect the lives of ordinary people in developing countries?
- What do you understand by the phrase *responsible tourism?*
- What can visitors do to ensure they are responsible tourists?

Spotlight 2
Useful language for talking about the past and generalizing

Expressions for referring to times in the past

1 **There are lots of words and phrases for expressing approximately when in the past an event occurred. Complete the sentences below using the words in the box.**

couple	few	just	long	other	recently	while

1 I was on a camping holiday ....
2 I was on a camping holiday a .... ago.
3 I was on a camping holiday a .... months ago.
4 The .... day, I was looking at a holiday brochure.
5 I was looking at a holiday brochure a .... of weeks ago.
6 I was looking at a holiday brochure .... a day or two ago.
7 I was looking at a holiday brochure not very .... ago.

Tip
Show the examiner your ability to be specific and accurate when referring to past time.

The impersonal *you*

> When describing typical experiences, it's often a good idea to use the impersonal *you*.
> For example, when talking about hotels:
> *In most hotels,* **you** *can't check in until the early afternoon, and* **you** *usually have to check out by around 11 a.m.*
> Some older grammar books suggest *one* as an alternative to the impersonal *you* (e.g. *One doesn't usually need to make a reservation.*). This is now considered very old-fashioned and is seldom used in spoken English.

2 Rewrite these sentences using the impersonal *you*.

1 It's possible to eat cheaply and very well in the local restaurants.
   you can eat cheaply and very well in the local restaurants.
2 It's necessary to book accommodation a long time in advance.
3 It's not a good idea to take a car into the city centre.
4 It's possible to use an international credit card to pay for most things.

Reported speech

> If you want to include something somebody said to you, remember the rules of reported speech. Verbs usually go into the past. However, for something which is obviously still true, putting the verb into the past can be optional.
>
> (We had a great time.)
>
> They said (that) they (had) had a great time.
>
> (The sea's freezing!)
>
> She said (that) the sea was freezing.
>
> (We love it here.)
>
> They said (that) they loved it there. / They said (that) they love it here/there.
>
> (I hate flying.)
>
> He said (that) he hated flying. / He said (that) he hates flying.
>
> If in doubt, change the verb to the past!

3 Change these sentences into reported speech.

1 'I'm not very happy with the hotel.'
   She said …
2 'I can read a bit of the local language, but I can't communicate.'
   He said …
3 'I don't want to eat in international chain restaurants.'
   She said …
4 'We come here every year.'
   They said …
5 'We've been coming here for the last ten years.'
   They said …
6 'We've never been here before.'
   They told me …

Exam skills 2

Illustrating your point

1 Read the five model answers below and on page 78 and match them to these strategies (a–e).

   a Admit the limitations of your knowledge.
   b Combine two or more short answers to make one longer one.
   c Give one or two hypothetical scenarios to illustrate your point.
   d Include a brief personal anecdote to illustrate a point.
   e Include an example you've seen in the media to illustrate a point.

   1 *Why do you think tourism is so popular and still increasing in popularity?*
     I suppose people like to do something different and have a change from their normal daily life. I think it's human nature to be curious about other places. Maybe it's also a status symbol. It can sound quite impressive if you say, 'I've just come back from a three-week holiday in Mexico' or wherever else you've just been.

   2 *Do you think people always get what they were hoping for on holiday?*
     Well, holidays are supposed to be relaxing, but some types of holiday can be quite stressful. I'm not talking about lying on a beach all day and package holidays, obviously, but independent travel can be quite hard work, especially if something goes wrong. For example, if you have an accident and have to go to hospital, that can be unpleasant in your own country, but at least you know what to do. In a foreign country, where you may not speak the language, it can be an extremely difficult and stressful experience. Also, holiday brochures often show attractive photos but don't tell the whole story about the place. There could be a big, noisy building site right in front of the hotel, for example. That sort of thing can lead to disappointment.

   3 *Why is tourism so important to some economies?*
     Foreign tourists tend to spend quite a lot of money, so it can bring a lot of money into the economy from outside. For some poor countries, tourism can be their main source of foreign currency. I don't exactly understand why countries need foreign currency, but I'm not an economist!

4 *What environmental problems can be caused by tourism?*

The biggest problem is probably that planes are one of the causes of climate change, but there can be local problems, too. A couple of years ago, I went to Cyprus in high summer. There was always plenty of water in our hotel. The swimming pool was full, and you could have five showers a day if you wanted to. But then a local man I was talking to in a bar told me that water for the local people was frequently restricted to five or six hours a day. The tourists could have as much water as they liked, while the people who lived there had to manage without for most of the day! It seemed so unfair, because the hundreds of hotels on the island are one of the main reasons *why* there's a water shortage there.

5 *What can be done to reduce these environmental problems?*

I think people should be discouraged from flying long distances for short breaks. The other day, I saw an article in the travel section of a newspaper which suggested flying half way round the world to Vietnam for a four-day break. People should try to fly less often, and stay for longer when they do fly. For local problems, like the water shortage in Cyprus I mentioned before, perhaps tourist taxes could help. Quite a lot of countries already have these, but they're usually very low. These could be increased to raise more money for solving these problems.

www.CartoonStock.com

2 **Work in pairs. Put these features in order of importance (1 = most important), then compare your order with the one given in the answer key. There isn't one 'right' order, but some points are more important than others.**

The illustration (anecdote or something you've seen in the media) should ...

a be clearly explained.

b be genuinely interesting.

c be relevant to the question.

d be short.

e be something the examiner probably doesn't already know.

f use complex grammar.

Prepare and practise

3 **Student A is the person who asked the questions in *Try it first!* Exercise 1 on page 75.**
Student B is the person who asked the questions in *Try it first!* Exercise 2 on page 75.

Student A: On a separate piece of paper, write notes for a complex answer to each of the questions from Exercise 1. Try to use some of the language from this unit.

Student B: Do the same for the questions from Exercise 2.

4 **Repeat the two role-plays from the *Try it first!* section on page 75. For the first set of questions, Student B asks the questions and Student A answers, based on his/her written notes (but from memory rather than just reading them aloud).**

5 **Reverse roles and repeat with the second set of questions.**

Listen 2

1 🎧 🎧 **14** **Listen to a Speaking Part 3 conversation about travel and tourism. Answer these questions, based on what the candidate says.**

Questions 1–3

Which THREE of these problems relating to tourism does the candidate mention?

A pick-pocketing

B serious crime

C health problems

D natural disasters

E destruction of local cultures

F price increases for local people

Questions 4–5

For each question, choose the correct letter: A, B or C.

4 Before leaving home, visitors should find out about local

  A problems.

  B customs.

  C culture.

5 Visitors should try to

  A spend plenty of money.

  B think about who will receive the money they spend.

  C offer to pay higher prices than local people pay.

2 **Discuss these questions in pairs.**

- What are the benefits for visitors to a country of trying the local cuisine?
- Millions of people who visit foreign countries don't attempt to find out about or sample the local culture. Why do you think this is?
- Have you ever heard/thought about 'responsible tourism'?

Pronunciation focus: review

Tip
Poor pronunciation is a common reason for getting a disappointing result in the Speaking test. Practise, practise, practise ...

3 **Previously, you have listened to sentences from the recording then tried to copy them for pronunciation. This time, do it the other way round: read a sentence aloud, record it, then play the version on the CD. How close is it to your version?**

4 **Take the roles of examiner and candidate and practise speaking for Part 3 again, based on these questions, which explore more issues related to travel and tourism.**

- What are the advantages and disadvantages of very cheap flights on budget airlines?
- Do you think the number of visitors to some of the world's most popular places should be limited? Why? / Why not?
- What are the advantages and disadvantages of going on holiday somewhere close to where you live?

5 **Swap roles and repeat with these questions.**

- Why do you think so many people like to spend their holidays in a beach resort?
- What are the advantages and disadvantages of beach resorts as places to have a holiday?
- What are the advantages and disadvantages of going on holiday out of season?

Check and challenge

Talking about past experiences

CHECK   **Find three other ways to say *I went camping recently*.**

CHALLENGE   **Write a short essay about a holiday or other travel experience you had recently. Use vocabulary from this unit to be very specific about your experience.**

The impersonal *you*

CHECK   **Which of these sentences feature the impersonal *you*?**

1   You must be crazy to want to go there for a holiday.
2   You have to be very patient in restaurants at peak times.
3   You can rent a beach-front apartment for next to nothing out of season.
4   You can't stay in that hotel. It's fully booked for the whole summer.

CHALLENGE   **Here's a common saying which uses the impersonal *you*, and could be useful when talking about holiday experiences:**

You get what you pay for.

What do you think it means? When would you use it?

Reported speech

CHECK   **Correct the errors in these sentences.**

1   When we arrived at the hotel, my wife says she wants to go for a swim.
2   The receptionist said us that the swimming pool was closed.
3   I asked to the receptionist when the swimming pool will be open again.
4   He told to me he didn't knew the answer.

CHALLENGE   **Remember some real things that people have said to you recently, then write them as reported speech.**

Speaking strategies

CHECK   **Here are some strategies from this unit and from Unit 6 for making your answers more interesting. Can you fill in the missing words from memory?**

1   Start with an obvious idea, then add a less obvious, more .... idea.
2   .... the focus of the question, but make sure it still includes what the examiner asked.
3   Admit the .... of your knowledge.
4   Combine two or more .... answers to make one .... one.
5   Give one or two .... scenarios to illustrate your point.
6   Include a brief personal .... to illustrate a point.
7   Include an example you've seen in .... to illustrate a point.
8   Refer to an ongoing ....
9   Start with an exception or exceptions, then describe the general ....

CHALLENGE   **Work with a partner to complete the practice Speaking tests which follow this unit. Try to use some of the above strategies.**

Four practice Speaking test role-plays

> These role-plays cover more topics which may feature in the exam.
> Student A: You are the examiner. Ask the questions. Try to keep to the times given.
> Student B: You are the candidate. Answer the questions.

Speaking test 1

Part 1 (approximately 4 minutes)

In the first part, I'd like to ask you a few questions about yourself. Let's talk about what you do. Do you work, or are you a student?

If a student: What subject are you studying?

Why did you choose to study this subject?

What do you hope to do when you finish studying?

If working: What kind of work do you do?

Why did you choose this kind of work?

What kind of work do you want to do in the future?

Now let's talk about your weekends.
- What do you usually do at the weekends?
- What will you do next weekend?
- How important is it for you to relax at the weekend?
- Do you think you have enough free time for relaxing?

Now let's talk about clothes and fashion.
- Are clothes and fashion important for you? Why? / Why not?
- What kind of clothes do you usually wear?
- Are there some kinds of clothes that you don't like?
- Has the kind of clothing you like changed over the years?

Part 2 (3–4 minutes, including preparation time)

I'm going to give you a topic, and I'd like you to talk about it for one to two minutes. Before you talk, you have one minute to think about what you're going to say. You can make some notes if you wish. Here's some paper and a pencil to make some notes. Here's your topic. I'd like you to describe a festival which is important in your country.

> Describe a festival which is important in your country. You should say:
>   what this festival is
>   when it occurs
>   what you did the last time it occurred
> and explain what you like and dislike about this festival.

Now, remember that you have one to two minutes for this. Don't worry if I stop you. I'll tell you when the time is up. Can you start speaking now, please?

(After the talk) Do you enjoy festivals in general?

Part 3 (approximately 5 minutes)

We've been talking about festivals in your country, and I'd like to discuss with you some more general questions related to this.

Let's consider first of all the importance of national festivals.
- How important are festivals in your country?
- Are festivals becoming more important or less important in your country?
- Why do you think most places have festivals?

Let's move on from national festivals to private family celebrations.
- What are the main events that families celebrate in your country?
- In some places, people spend a lot of money on celebrating important family events. Do you think this is a good way to spend money?
- Do you think commercial interests influence what happens in family celebrations? If so, how?

Speaking test 2

Part 1 (approximately 4 minutes)

In the first part, I'd like to ask you a few questions about yourself. Let's talk about what you do. Do you work, or are you a student?

If a student: What subject are you studying?
                    How long have you studied this subject?
                    What do you like about studying this subject?

If working: What kind of work do you do?
                    How long have you done this kind of work?
                    What do you like about this kind of work?

Now let's talk about the weather.
- Have you ever been in very hot weather? (When was it?)
- How often is the weather very hot where you come from?
- Are some parts of your country hotter than others?
- Do you prefer hot weather or cold weather? Why?

Now let's talk about friends.
- Do you prefer to spend time with one friend or with a group of friends? Why? / Why not?
- What do you like doing when you are with a friend or friends?
- How do you usually contact your friends?
- How important are friends in your life?

Part 2 (3–4 minutes, including preparation time)

I'm going to give you a topic, and I'd like you to talk about it for one to two minutes. Before you talk, you have one minute to think about what you're going to say. You can make some notes if you wish. Here's some paper and a pencil to make some notes. Here's your topic. I'd like you to describe a sport or game you enjoy playing.

> Describe a sport or game you enjoy playing. You should say:
>   what the sport or game is
>   when and where you play it
>   who you play it with
> and explain why you like playing it.

Now, remember that you have one to two minutes for this. Don't worry if I stop you. I'll tell you when the time is up. Can you start speaking now, please?

(After the talk) How often do you play *(sport/game the candidate chose)*?
                  When will you next play *(sport/game the candidate chose)*?

Part 3 (approximately 5 minutes)

We've been talking about sports and games, and I'd like to discuss with you some more general questions related to this.
- Do you think it's important for children to spend time doing sports? Why? / Why not?
- Do you think competitive games for children are a good thing or a bad thing?
- Why do you think children enjoy games?

Let's move on from sport for children to major sporting events.
- How important are sporting events in your country?
- Why do you think that watching sports is such a popular activity?
- What are the advantages and disadvantages of watching sporting events live rather than on TV?

Speaking test 3

Part 1 (approximately 4 minutes)

In the first part, I'd like to ask you a few questions about yourself. Let's talk about what you do. Do you work, or are you a student?

If a student:	What subject are you studying?
	What do you like about studying this subject?
	Is there anything you dislike about studying this subject?
If working:	What kind of work do you do?
	What do you like about this kind of work?
	Is there anything you dislike about this kind of work?

Now let's talk about pets.
- Do you have a pet or pets at home? (What is it / are they?)
- What do you enjoy about having a pet?
- Which animals are most popular as pets in your country?
- In most places, dogs are the most popular pets. Why do you think this is?

Now let's talk about the countryside.
- Do you enjoy being in the countryside? Why? / Why not?
- How often do you spend time in the countryside?
- What do you like doing when you are in the countryside?
- Why do you think that many people who live in cities enjoy visiting the countryside?

Part 2 (3–4 minutes, including preparation time)

I'm going to give you a topic, and I'd like you to talk about it for one to two minutes. Before you talk, you have one minute to think about what you're going to say. You can make some notes if you wish. Here's some paper and a pencil to make some notes. Here's your topic. I'd like you to describe a piece of electronic equipment you find useful.

> Describe a piece of electronic equipment you find useful. You should say:
>   what it is
>   how long you have owned it
>   why you find it useful
> and explain how your life would be different without it.

Now, remember that you have one to two minutes for this. Don't worry if I stop you. I'll tell you when the time is up. Can you start speaking now, please?

(After the talk) How long have you had your *(item the candidate chose)*?
                 Would you get another one if you lost it?

Part 3 (approximately 5 minutes)

We've been talking about technology, and I'd like to discuss with you some more general questions related to this.
- Why do you think mobile phones are so popular?
- How has the way people use mobile phones changed over the years?
- What are the advantages and disadvantages of speaking face to face rather than on the telephone?

Let's move on from the telephone to technology in general.
- Why do you think so many people want to own the latest technology?
- Do you think we are becoming too dependent on technology?
- Do you think that eventually technology will be able to solve every problem?

Speaking test 4

Part 1 (approximately 4 minutes)

In the first part, I'd like to ask you a few questions about yourself. Let's talk about what you do. Do you work, or are you a student?

If a student: What subject are you studying?

What do you hope to do when you finish studying?

Why do you hope to do this?

If working: What kind of work do you do?

What kind of work would you like to do in the future?

Why would you like to do this?

Now let's talk about food.

- What kind of food do you enjoy?
- How often do you cook?
- How important are meal times in your home?
- Do you enjoy going to restaurants? Why? / Why not?

Now let's talk about gifts.

- When do people give each other gifts where you come from?
- Is it usual to bring a gift when you visit another person's home?
- How important are gifts in your culture?
- What kinds of gift do you like receiving?

Part 2 (3–4 minutes, including preparation time)

I'm going to give you a topic, and I'd like you to talk about it for one to two minutes. Before you talk, you have one minute to think about what you're going to say. You can make some notes if you wish. Here's some paper and a pencil to make some notes. Here's your topic. I'd like you to describe a person who has done something you admire.

> Describe a person who has done something you admire. You should say:
>   who this person is
>   how famous this person is
>   what this person has done
> and explain why you admire this person.

Now, remember that you have one to two minutes for this. Don't worry if I stop you. I'll tell you when the time is up. Can you start speaking now, please?

(After the talk, if the person is a celebrity) Would you like to meet this person?
(If the person is not famous) When did you last meet this person?
                              Will you be meeting this person again soon?

Part 3 (approximately 5 minutes)

We've been talking about a person you admire, and I'd like to discuss with you some more general questions related to this.

- What kind of people are most likely to become famous?
- Do you think people become famous for the right reasons?
- How easy is it to become famous? Do you think that fame can be bought?

Let's move on from reasons for becoming famous to fame in general.

- What are the advantages and disadvantages of being famous?
- Why do you think so many ordinary people are interested in the lives of famous people?
- Do you think we have become too interested in the lives of the famous?

UNIT 8 # Getting things sorted out

LISTENING SECTION 1: SOCIAL NEEDS – CONVERSATION

Section 1 of the Listening test is a conversation between two people relating to social and commercial needs. It is often based on a speaker finding out information about an event, arrangements for a job, travel arrangements or an everyday commercial transaction, such as buying insurance over the telephone.

There is only one conversation, but it often has phases. For example, in the first phase, a woman phones to find out about buying theatre tickets; in the second phase, she gives her name, address and credit-card details so the tickets can be posted to her.

There are ten questions, and these may use any of the Listening test formats.

Spotlight 1
Addresses and numbers

1 **Address formats vary from country to country. When addresses feature in the IELTS Listening test, they are usually in the British format. Rewrite the lines of this address in the correct order.**

a Beaminster	**c** DT8 3BW	**e** 14 Monmouth Road
b United Kingdom	**d** Garner House	**f** Flat 3

2 **It can be helpful to know the format of certain other types of information likely to occur in the recording. For each pair in items 1–4, choose the correct format. For items 5–7, choose the option that is *not* correct.**

1 credit-card number
   a 4478 3772 8574 9910
   b 4478 3772 8574

2 train-ticket price
   a €17.80 to go, €32.20 to return
   b €17.80 one way, €32.20 return

3 journey times
   a The journey takes three hours, 45 minutes.
   b The journey takes 45 minutes and three hours.

Tip
Spellings, numbers and dates are very likely to occur in Section 1. Make sure you are confident about listening to and writing down letters of the alphabet and numbers. Some are easily confused with each other when heard quickly (for example, 40 and 14, or P and B). You could practise dictating spellings and numbers with a friend.

4 **decimal points**

2.75 is said as ...

  a two point seven five

  b two point seventy-five

5 **Which one of these ways to say the telephone number 622010 is *not* correct?**

  a six double two oh one oh

  b six two two oh one oh

  c six two two nought one nought

  d six two two zero one zero

6 **Which one of these ways to say the date 23rd April is *not* correct?**

  a the twenty-third of April

  b twenty-three of April

  c April the twenty-third

  d April twenty-third

  e twenty-three, four

7 **Which one of these ways to say the price $19.90 is *not* correct?**

  a nineteen dollars ninety

  b nineteen dollars and ninety cents

  c nineteen ninety

  d nineteen dollars, ninety cents

  e nineteen ninety dollars

Predicting and practising 1
Detailed information

Tip
Section 1 recordings are often based on exchanging information about personal and practical details. Predicting the type of information required and knowing the usual format will help you in the exam.

The Listening test gets progressively more difficult, so Section 1 is the easiest part. If you are hoping to get 6.5 or higher in the whole exam, aim to get 100% correct in Listening Sections 1 and 2.

1 **Complete the details on the forms below with any example information you wish. Base the formats on your knowledge of the world. For example, how many digits does a credit-card number have? How long is a hotel booking likely to be? How much is a theatre ticket likely to cost in euros? Work in pairs if possible.**

Name: ....

Address: ....

....

....

Telephone number: ....

Credit-card number: .... Expiry date: ...... / ......

Hotel booking dates: .... to ....

Room type: ....

Tip
Predicting the answers will help you in all parts of the Listening test. There are two main types of prediction: predicting the type of information required, and predicting the likely range of possible answers.

Theatre ticket prices: Stalls rows A to H: ....

                                Stalls rows J to W: ....

                                Circle: ....

Start time: ....

2 🎧 **15** Listen to four conversations, and fill in the missing information.

Name: **1** ....

Address: **2** ....

....

....

Telephone number: **3** ....

Credit-card number: **4** .... Expiry date: **5** .... / ....

Hotel booking dates: **6** .... to ....

Room type: **7** ....

Theatre ticket prices: Stalls rows A to H: **8** ....

Stalls rows J to W: **9** ....

Circle: **10** ....

Start time: **11** ....

3 Compare the information in Exercise 2 with the information you wrote in Exercise 1. What similarities do you notice?

4 🎧 **16** Now listen to a Section 1 extract and complete this exam question.

*Complete the form below. Write **NO MORE THAN ONE WORD AND/OR A NUMBER** for each answer.*

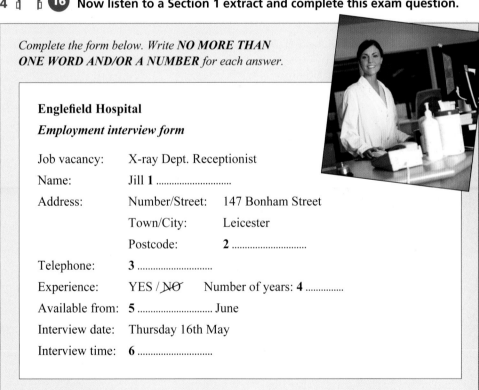

Englefield Hospital

Employment interview form

Job vacancy: X-ray Dept. Receptionist

Name: Jill **1** ....

Address: Number/Street: 147 Bonham Street

Town/City: Leicester

Postcode: **2** ....

Telephone: **3** ....

Experience: YES / N̶O̶   Number of years: **4** ....

Available from: **5** .... June

Interview date: Thursday 16th May

Interview time: **6** ....

Focus on formats 1: form completion

The form-completion format above can, like all the listening formats, appear in any part of the Listening test, but it is especially common in Section 1. It is likely to require details of names, addresses, times, dates, etc. (although any type of information could be required).

Predicting and practising 2
General information

> Section 1 doesn't only feature detailed information such as addresses, prices, times, etc. It normally also features questions about the general situation in which the conversation occurs, and about the results of that conversation. Again, predicting the type of information you will need to listen for can help you in the exam.

1 Predict possible answers for these situations and questions.

1 A student wants to insure her possessions. What does the insurance *not* cover?
2 A man is looking for accommodation to rent. What type of accommodation does he want?
3 Two people are choosing a restaurant for a business lunch. What's the most important thing about the restaurant they choose?

2 🎧 **17** **Listen to three short extracts and complete this exam question. Were your guesses in Exercise 1 close to the correct answers?**

> *Complete the notes below. Write **NO MORE THAN THREE WORDS** for each answer.*
>
> **1** Insurance does not cover: ....
> **2** Type of accommodation: ....
> **3** The most important factor in choosing the restaurant is that it must be ....

3 Look at the exam question below and answer these questions.

1 What kind of trip is it? (clues: *coach, child, school, parents*)
2 What are typical destinations for school trips? (Question 1)
3 In what kind of places could a coach wait? (Question 2)
4 What do children typically need to take on a school trip? (Question 3)
5 What information might parents need about the trip? (Question 4)

'And that's why we make 'em sign permission slips.'

> *Complete the sentences below. Write **NO MORE THAN THREE WORDS** for each answer.*
>
> The trip is to Whitsmead **1** ....
> The coach leaves at 8 a.m. from the **2** .... next to the school.
> Each child needs to take **3** ....
> The school will phone to tell parents the **4** ....

4 🎧 **18** **Now listen to a longer Section 1 extract and complete the exam question in Exercise 3.**

Tip
In Section 1 questions based on writing words in spaces, you will always hear the exact words you need to write.

Focus on formats 2: sentence completion, note completion, table completion and short answers

● The **note-completion** and **sentence-completion** examples on page 88 ask for 'no more than three words', but other instructions are possible, such as 'no more than one word or a number' and 'no more than two words and/or a number'.
● The **table-completion** format is similar, but requires information which is more clearly arranged in table form.
● The **short-answer** format is similar to note completion, but is in question-and-answer format instead:

*Answer below. Write **NO MORE THAN THREE WORDS** for each answer.*

1 What does the insurance <u>not</u> cover? ....

2 What type of accommodation is the man looking for? ....

3 Where must the restaurant be? ....

5 How well are you prepared for the exam formats? Decide whether these statements are true (T) or false (F).

1 'Write NO MORE THAN THREE WORDS for each answer' means you will lose marks if you write more than three words.

2 'Write NO MORE THAN THREE WORDS AND/OR A NUMBER for each answer' means you can write any combination of up to four words and numbers for each answer.

3 In formats requiring you to write in words, there is not necessarily only one possibility. There may be one or more acceptable alternatives.

4 The formats described in the box above only occur in Sections 1 and 2.

5 In Section 1, you hear all of the recording twice. In Sections 2, 3 and 4, you only hear the recording once.

6 You must complete your final answer sheet at the same time as you listen.

7 Most people think Section 1 is much easier than Section 4.

The full-length Section 1 Listening test on page 90 combines table completion with a note-completion task.

Preparing to answer 1

For each section in the exam, you will first hear the situation of the recording. In this case:

You will hear two people discussing travel arrangements from an airport to a city centre.

Then you will have a short time (around 20 seconds) to look at the questions. You will be asked to look at approximately half the questions, in this case Questions 1–5.
In Section 1, you will hear the part of the recording relating to the example first. Then you hear all the recording from the beginning to the end of the questions you were asked to look at. The recording will then stop and you will have short time look at the rest of the questions before the recording starts again.

Tip
With only 20 seconds, you won't have time to consider the questions in great detail, but combining what you have already heard with what you can deduce from reading the questions can be very helpful.

1 Look at Questions 1 to 5 in the exam task below. What type of information is needed in each gap?

2 Now look at Questions 6–10. What can you guess about the situation to help you listen for the information you need? What is the range of possible answers for each question?

3 🎧 **19** Now listen and do the exam task.

Questions 1–5

Complete the table below. Write **NO MORE THAN ONE WORD AND/OR A NUMBER** *for each answer.*

	Frequency	Journey takes	Cost	Operates
train	every 30 minutes	Example: 12 minutes	1	5 a.m. – 11.45 p.m.
bus	every 2	3	$11	24 hours
taxi	on demand	approximately 4	$38	5 ....

Questions 6–10

Complete the notes below. Write **NO MORE THAN THREE WORDS AND/OR A NUMBER** *for each answer.*

Office closed after **6** ....
To call taxi, phone when **7** ....
*Taxi waiting by sign saying '***8** ....'.
Pay driver in cash.
Cash machine at the airport.
Show driver the **9** ....
Email address: **10** ....

In this section, you have looked at question formats which require you to write in missing information, but remember: ANY QUESTION FORMAT CAN BE USED IN ANY SECTION.

LISTENING SECTION 2: SOCIAL NEEDS – MONOLOGUE

Section 2 is a monologue relating to social needs and arrangements. It is often based on a speaker giving information to an audience about the practical arrangements for an event, or the facilities of an institution such as a college or business hotel. The level of difficulty is slightly higher than Section 1. There are ten questions, and these may use any of the Listening test formats. In Section 2, you may have to listen to directions and identify parts of a map, or listen to a description of a place and match parts of it with locations on a map.

Spotlight 2
Directions and locations

1 For each sentence, choose the correct option. In some sentences, both options are correct.

1 After about 20 metres, turn right *in / into* Hedge Street.
2 Then go straight on until you *come / arrive* to some traffic lights.
3 From the main entrance, go *pass / past* the ticket office and into the café.
4 Walk *down / along* the corridor, all the way to the end.
5 Go *up / down* the stairs and when you get to the landing, you'll see a small door.
6 Go *over / round* the bridge and park wherever you can find a space.
7 Take a left turn *at / on* the corner of the street.
8 It only takes a few minutes to walk *across / through* the park.

2 Complete the sentences below with the words and phrases in the box.

adjoining	away	enter via	is divided into
is on the far side of		leading from	nearby	runs alongside

1 Visitors can .... the main gate or the side gate in Easton Lane.
2 The path .... the sports ground for about 100 metres.
3 The seating .... three zones.
4 There's a picnic area .... the main part of the wildlife park.
5 The ticket office .... the car park.
6 There's a footpath .... the water tower to the barbecue area.
7 The information office is just a few metres ....
8 You can get a snack or cup of coffee in the café ....

Predicting and practising 3
Labelling a map

1 Look at the map and the text that goes with it in the exam question below. What do you know about holiday villages? What features do they tend to have? Where do they tend to be located? If you've never visited one, what do you imagine they are like? Can you guess what any parts of the map are?

2 🎧 **20** Listen to the recording and do the exam task. When you have finished, read the audio transcript on page 112 and underline all the language which describes where things are relative to other things on the map.

Questions 11–15

*Look at the plan of the holiday village below. Choose **FIVE** answers from the box and write the correct letter, **A–F**, next to questions **11–15**.*

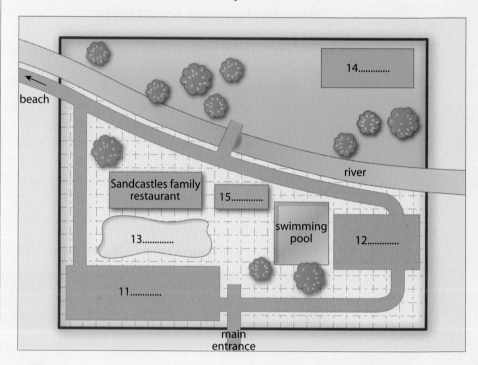

A Sea Breeze restaurant and bar

B barbecue area

C children's play area

D shop

E main car park

F overflow car park

Focus on formats 3: map labelling and matching
The map-labelling task format requires you to identify the parts of the map by understanding a description of their locations. The parts are numbered in the order that you will hear them in the recording. A second type of map-labelling task requires you to identify places on a map by following directions. The full-length Section 2 Listening test on page 93 combines this type of map-labelling task with another form of task based on matching: you have to match text with text.

Preparing to answer 2

1 Look very briefly at Questions 11–15 in the exam task below and answer these questions.

    1 Will the talk be about an event, a place or a building development?

    2 Are there more options than questions, or vice versa?

2 Now look very briefly at Questions 16–20 and answer these questions.

    1 Are there more options than questions, or vice versa?

    2 What is the theme linking the questions?

3 🎧 21 Now listen and do the exam task.

Questions 11–15

*Look at the plan of the boat show below. Write the correct letter, **A–F**, next to questions 11–15.*

11 electronic notice-board ....

12 first-aid station ....

13 food and drinks stall ....

14 cash machines ....

15 equipment and supplies stands ....

Questions 16–20

What does the speaker say about the arrangements for this year's show?

*Write the correct letter, **A**, **B** or **C**, next to questions 16–20.*

A will cost more than last year

B will stay the same price

C will cost less than last year

Arrangements

16 Paper tickets ....

17 Electronic tickets ....

18 Exhibiting at the show ....

19 The show brochure ....

20 The show shuttle bus ....

Check and challenge

Writing and saying names, dates, times, numbers, etc.

CHECK
1 Give three different ways to *say* the date of your birthday.
2 Give three different ways to *write* the date of your birthday.
3 Give three different ways to *say* the time it is right now.
4 Give three different ways to *write* the time it is right now.

CHALLENGE
Working with a partner, dictate and write personal names, place names, dates, times, phone numbers and other practical information associated with Listening Section 1. How do the written forms relate to the spoken forms?

The exam format

CHECK
Decide whether these statements about Listening Sections 1 and 2 are true (T) or false (F).
1 Section 1 is played twice.
2 Section 1 may feature one, two or three speakers.
3 Section 2 is played once.
4 Section 2 will probably seem a little more difficult than Section 1.
5 Instructions such as 'Write no more than three words' are a suggestion. It doesn't matter if you write more.
6 Section 2 always includes a map-labelling task.
7 In both Sections 1 and 2, you are given two pauses to read the questions.

CHALLENGE
Use this book and other sources, such as the official IELTS website (www.ielts.org), to make sure that you are really familiar with the format of the exam, that you know exactly what to expect, and that you know the requirements for each question format. Don't lose points by misunderstanding what you have to do!

UNIT 9 ▸ Looking at the bigger picture

LISTENING SECTION 3: ACADEMIC/ TRAINING NEEDS – CONVERSATION

Section 3 is a conversation between two or more people relating to education or training. Here are some examples:

- A lecturer goes over an essay with a student, discussing its strengths and weaknesses.
- A tutor discusses selecting courses with a student, commenting on the advantages and disadvantages of various options.
- Two students discuss a problem with the structure of their course.
- Three students discuss plans to improve their academic work.

There is only one conversation, but it is divided into two parts. There are ten questions, and these may use any of the Listening test formats.

The Listening test gets progressively more difficult, so Section 3 will probably seem noticeably more difficult than Section 2 and a lot more difficult than Section 1. It's not unusual to get 6.5 to 7.5 in the whole exam without getting 100% correct in Sections 3 and 4. But that doesn't mean you shouldn't try your very best, of course!

Spotlight 1
Language for talking about study

1 Discuss the differences in meaning between these sets of words.

1 examinations / tests	9 to pass / to graduate
2 grades / points	10 to mark an essay / to check an essay
3 a subject / a course	11 a lecture / a seminar
4 a tutorial / an interview	12 a graduate / an undergraduate
5 a teacher / a lecturer	13 a professor / a tutor
6 to teach / to train	14 academic / educational
7 an essay / a dissertation	15 a Master's degree / a postgraduate degree
8 evidence / argument	16 a discussion / a debate / a talk

2 Choose the correct option to complete each of these sentences.

1 My final *examinations / tests* are next summer. Then I'll be a graduate, assuming I pass.

2 My son isn't particularly *academic / educational*, and doesn't want to go to university.

3 Unfortunately, I didn't get very good *grades / points* last year.

4 In the *seminar / lecture*, we discussed the importance of international trade. Some people made useful points, but I didn't say much.

5 I had to spend all weekend *marking / checking* my students' essays, and most of them were terrible. Nobody got more than a C+.

6 I'm doing a postgraduate *subject / course* in Development Studies.

7 Boreham Hall is a *teacher-training / teacher-teaching* college.

8 My *essay / dissertation* is nearly 30,000 words, and it took me four months to write.

9 I have to discuss my course options with my personal *professor / tutor*.

10 You need to supply more *evidence / arguments* to support your *evidence / argument*.

3 Complete each of the sentences below using the correct form of a phrasal verb from the box.

catch up	drop out	fall behind	fill out/in	go over
hand back	hand in	leave out	pick up	work out

1 I need to .... this essay again to make sure I haven't left out any important points.

2 Jack had lots of personal problems, so he .... of college half way through his second year.

3 Could you .... this form with your personal details, please?

4 When you're planning an essay, try to .... any ideas which are not relevant to the argument.

5 If you haven't yet given me your end-of-term essays, please .... them .... by 5 p.m. tomorrow at the very latest.

6 Hitomi never studied English formally in college. She just .... it .... when she was living in Australia.

7 It's a good idea to try to .... the meaning of a word from its context before you use your dictionary.

8 I was off sick for two weeks, so I had to work hard to .... with all the work I missed.

9 If you don't go to the lectures, you'll .... with the work, and the other students will be ahead of you.

10 The essays will be marked and .... to you on or around May 3rd.

Tip
Language for talking about study and educational institutions is very likely to occur in Section 3.

Focus on formats 1

Multiple choice: matching the question with the correct information

1 Look at this multiple-choice question and the extract below from a Section 3 recording. The correct answer is B, but notice how the mentions of rocks and fish (see underlined text) could distract you from choosing the correct answer. You have to understand the whole conversation, not just listen for key words.

---

*Choose the correct letter, **A**, **B** or **C**.*

What did the student bring back from the field trip?

A A geological sample

B Some samples of a rare plant

C Some fish

Tutor: How was the field trip to the lake?
Student: It went really well. The weather wasn't fantastic, but it didn't matter too much. We all had waterproof clothing. It's a really beautiful place, with amazing <u>rock formations</u>.
Tutor: Yes, it is. I've been there a few times. It's an amazing place. And did you get what you went for?
Student: Yes, we did. Although it was quite windy, it was safe enough to take a boat out, and we got some good <u>samples of the pond weed which is only known to occur in the deeper parts of that lake.</u>
Tutor: And did you catch any <u>fish</u>?
Student: Well, we did see one or two, but that's not what we were after.

Multiple choice: completing a sentence

2 The format in Exercise 1 above is basic multiple choice, and you have probably seen this in many other contexts. The IELTS exam also uses other multiple-choice formats. Look at this exam task and underline the information in the recording extract below you need to answer the question. Also underline the information that could tempt you into choosing the wrong answer.

---

*Choose the correct letter, **A**, **B** or **C**.*

The students are going to work on the project together because

A there is too much work for one person.

B it will be easier.

C they think it will be more interesting to collaborate.

Anna: Hi, Tony. It's great that we're allowed to collaborate on this project. It'll be much better than working on it individually.
Tony: Absolutely. And there's going to be a lot of data to process here. It's going to take hours, even with two of us. I don't think somebody working alone could do it in the time.
Anna: Would it be easier to work on all of it together, or take half each?
Tony: Well, it would be more interesting to work on all of it together, but it would be quicker to do half each, and we don't have a lot of time.

Multiple choice: choose two or more from a list

3 **22** **Now look at this third multiple-choice format. Listen and choose the correct answers.**

*Choose the correct letters, **A** to **E**.*

*Which **TWO** courses is the student going to choose for the next semester?*

A Twentieth-century American novels

B Nineteenth-century poetry

C Medieval poetry

D Contemporary poetry

E Contemporary American novels

Spotlight 2

Language for agreeing and disagreeing

In Section 3, identifying the correct answer often depends on understanding whether somebody has agreed or disagreed with what was said before.

For each of these utterances, do you think that the tutor agrees with what the student has just said (A), disagrees (D) or isn't sure (NS)?

1 I'm not sure about that.

2 I see what you mean, but …

3 Absolutely./Definitely.

4 That's not really the point though, is it?

5 You've hit the nail on the head.

6 That's one way of looking at it.

7 I do see your point. However, …

8 I suppose so.

9 That may be so, but on the other hand …

10 Well, yes, but that's not really what I meant.

Preparing to answer 1

1 The full-length Section 3 task below uses two of the multiple-choice formats shown on pages 97–98, plus the short-answer format which you saw in Unit 8. Look briefly at the seven sentences (A–G) in Questions 21–23 – how well can you remember them? When you listen, you may find it helpful to cross out the answers which are not true.

2 🎧 **23** Now listen and answer Questions 21–30.

Tip
Long lists of sentences like this can look difficult, but they are dealt with in the recording in same order as they are shown on the page. If you miss one, leave it and concentrate on the next. You may be able to guess the answer later by a process of elimination. (For example, if A and B are correct, and C, D, E and G are not correct, then F must be correct too.)

SECTION 3

Questions 21–23

*Choose the correct letters, **A** to **G**.*

*Which **THREE** problems does the tutor identify in the student's essay?*

A   The arguments are not supported by evidence.
B   The structure is not very good.
C   It is too similar to essays the student has read.
D   There are too many personal points of view.
E   The style is too formal and academic.
F   The paragraphs should be shorter.
G   The essay should be longer.

21 ....
22 ....
23 ....

Questions 24 and 25

*Choose the correct letter, **A**, **B** or **C**.*

24 The tutor says that in academic books, paragraphs are
  A usually very long.
  B occasionally very long.
  C usually shorter than paragraphs written by undergraduates.

25 The tutor says Alex's paragraphs should usually be
  A no longer than 400 words.
  B around 200 words.
  C 200 to 400 words.

Questions 26–30

*Answer the questions below. Write **NO MORE THAN THREE WORDS** for each answer.*

26 Where is the error in Alex's essay? ....
27 What are the scientists in Antarctica collecting? ....
28 What has ESSCOM been searching for in Antarctica? ....
29 What has the tutor's university been researching in Antarctica? ....
30 How has the region been mapped? ....

Tip
Unlike multiple-choice questions, for short-answer questions you will normally hear the exact words you need.

LISTENING SECTION 4: LECTURE OR FORMAL TALK

Section 4 is a monologue in the form of a lecture, talk or other type of presentation on an academic subject. It is generally considered to be the most difficult part of the Listening test. Unlike the other sections, there is no break in the middle for looking at the questions, but there are a number of very short pauses to allow you a moment to think about your answers. There are ten questions, and these may use any of the Listening test formats.

Spotlight 3
Academic English

1 Say whether each of these features is more associated with academic English or informal English.

1 Using contractions (*isn't, didn't, won't*, etc.)
2 Using *I, me, my, you* and *your*
3 Using the passive form a lot
4 Giving personal information and opinions
5 Quoting what other people have said
6 Quoting what other people have written
7 Using a lot of long words
8 Using long sentences
9 Explaining complex processes with chains of cause and effect

2 Put these words and phrases in the correct column of the table below according to the form of English they are associated with.

boss   consists of   doing a degree   founded   governed by
I think   institution   known as   lots of   principally   really good
specializing in   stuff   substance   undoubtedly

formal/academic	informal

> **Tip**
> Listening Section 4 often requires you to understand more formal varieties of English, such as you would hear in an academic lecture. Some parts may be quite close to written academic English. Whenever you see or hear examples of English, try to understand the level of formality of the language being used.

3 Discuss these questions in pairs or small groups.

- Why do we have these two forms of English?
- How clear is the boundary between the two types?
- What differences are there between formal **spoken** English and formal **written** English?
- How can you know if a word or phrase is usually formal or informal?
- What can you do to get more experience of listening to talks and lectures in informal English?

'Brachiating?! Kids these days ... whatever happened to good old fashioned swinging?!'

www.CartoonStock.com

Spotlight 4
Language for describing processes

Complete the sentences below with the phrases in the box.

After that	Prior to	The end result
The next stage		To begin with

1 .... , you need to hire an architect to design the new building.

2 .... is to get planning permission from the local authorities.

3 .... , you can start negotiating with contractors to do the building work.

4 .... signing the contracts with the contractors, you should consult a lawyer.

5 .... should be a smooth construction process.

Focus on formats 2

Flow charts

1 Look at the extract on page 102 from a Section 3 recording. Underline the parts of the script that supply the information you need and complete this chart.

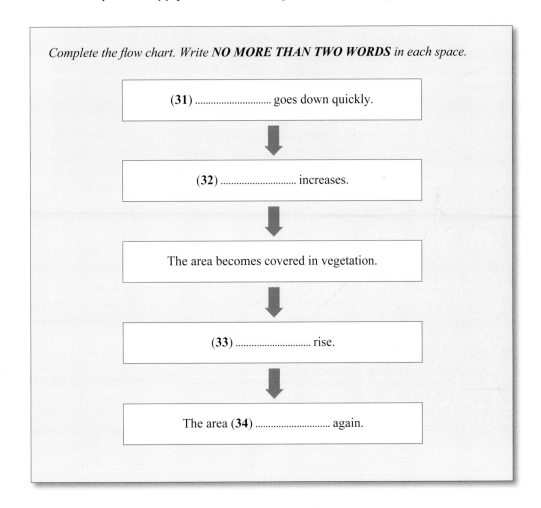

Complete the flow chart. Write **NO MORE THAN TWO WORDS** *in each space.*

(31) .... goes down quickly.

↓

(32) .... increases.

↓

The area becomes covered in vegetation.

↓

(33) .... rise.

↓

The area (34) .... again.

A common myth about the Sahara is that this desolate landscape used to be lushly fertile agricultural land, but due to over-farming by its inhabitants, it eventually became desert. It's true that around 12,000 years ago, much of the region was covered in tropical vegetation and supported a substantial human population, but a few thousand years earlier than that, the desert was even larger than it is today.

Human activity has undoubtedly affected the boundaries of the Sahara, principally through the cutting down of trees and bushes for use as fuel, but the main cause of its expansion and contraction over time is probably due to a process known as the 'Sahara Pump'. So what is the Sahara Pump? Well, it certainly isn't a machine for inflating tyres! This theory says that at various points over geological time, the temperature of the Sahara region falls relatively fast. Of course, in geological terms, 'fast' means over thousands of years. This allows greater rainfall, leading to so-called 'Green Sahara' periods. Those are periods when the region is covered in vegetation. However, the same process continues, and temperatures then start to go up again. Of course, this means that the region starts to dry out and eventually reverts to desert, which is the phase it is in at the moment. Even today, though,

temperatures can vary considerably. For example, one February day in 1979, people in southern Algeria, well inside the boundary of the desert, were going about their business as usual when they noticed a strange white substance floating in the air. Snow was falling!

Summary completion

Tip
Section 4 is difficult, and very few IELTS candidates understand every word they hear in this part. If you haven't understood, you may be able to use your knowledge of the world to make an 'educated guess'. And never leave an answer blank!

2 🎧 **24** **Another format is summary completion, and this can also be used to test understanding of processes and sequences of events. Listen to a continuation of the talk from Exercise 1 and complete the summary in this exam task.**

Complete the summary below. Write **NO MORE THAN TWO WORDS** *in each space.*

There used to be very few **(35)** .... in the region, but the numbers have increased recently. This has increased the demand for **(36)** .... Awareness of the problem this causes is **(37)** .... , but many visitors have little respect for the needs of **(38)** ....

Preparing to answer 2

> This is a full-length Section 4 task which uses the summary-completion and flow-chart formats shown on pages 101–102, plus one of the multiple-choice formats you looked at earlier in this unit.

1 Look briefly at the questions. Will your knowledge of the world help you to guess possible answers if you don't fully understand the recording? Can you predict ranges of possible answers for some questions?

2 🎧 **25** Now listen and answer the questions.

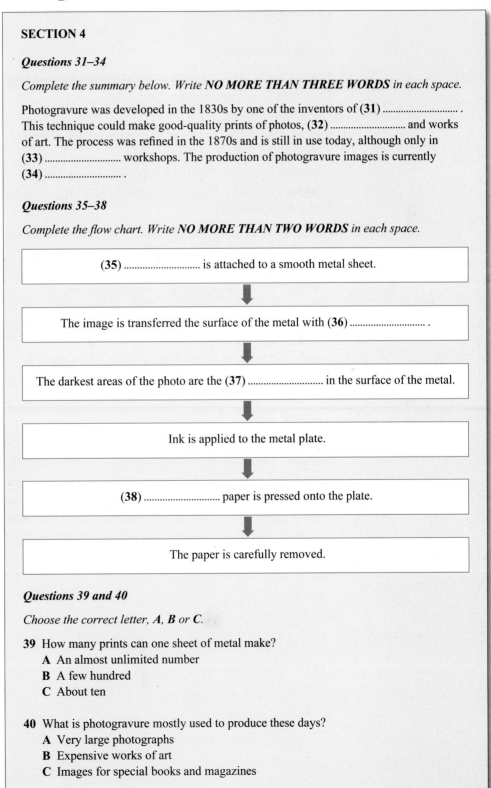

SECTION 4

Questions 31–34

Complete the summary below. Write **NO MORE THAN THREE WORDS** *in each space.*

Photogravure was developed in the 1830s by one of the inventors of **(31)** .... This technique could make good-quality prints of photos, **(32)** .... and works of art. The process was refined in the 1870s and is still in use today, although only in **(33)** .... workshops. The production of photogravure images is currently **(34)** ....

Questions 35–38

Complete the flow chart. Write **NO MORE THAN TWO WORDS** *in each space.*

(35) .... is attached to a smooth metal sheet.

⬇

The image is transferred the surface of the metal with **(36)** ....

⬇

The darkest areas of the photo are the **(37)** .... in the surface of the metal.

⬇

Ink is applied to the metal plate.

⬇

(38) .... paper is pressed onto the plate.

⬇

The paper is carefully removed.

Questions 39 and 40

Choose the correct letter, A, B or C.

39 How many prints can one sheet of metal make?
   A An almost unlimited number
   B A few hundred
   C About ten

40 What is photogravure mostly used to produce these days?
   A Very large photographs
   B Expensive works of art
   C Images for special books and magazines

Check and challenge

Talking about past experiences

CHECK **Write five ways students can prove to tutors what they have learned.**

CHALLENGE **If you are or have been a student in higher education, write a short essay about your experiences of dealing with academic staff. Answer these questions.**

- How did you choose which aspects of the subject to study?
- How was your progress assessed?
- How much involvement did members of staff have in directing your studies?
- Are there any changes which would have helped you study more effectively?

If you have never been a student, imagine the day of a university lecturer. What do you think he/she does?

Academic English

CHECK **Rewrite these sentences in a more academic type of English.**

1 The college got off the ground in 1920.

2 The way this essay is put together isn't great.

Now rewrite these sentences in a more informal type of English.

3 The courses are of very high quality.

4 I am of the opinion that the school-leaving age should be raised.

The exam format

CHECK **Decide whether these statements about Listening Sections 3 and 4 are true (T) or false (F).**

1 Section 3 is always a conversation between a tutor and a student.

2 Section 4 is always one person talking to an audience.

3 There are only two types of multiple-choice question.

4 In flow-chart and summary-completion tasks for Sections 3 and 4, the exact words you need are heard in the recording.

5 It's very difficult for lower-level students to score any points at all in Section 4.

6 In both Sections 3 and 4, you are given two pauses to read the questions.

7 At the end of the test, you have five minutes to transfer your answers to the answer sheet.

CHALLENGE **Visit www.ted.com.**

This website is a superb resource of lectures to watch and listen to. *TED* stands for Technology, Entertainment, Design, but the talks cover a very wide range of themes, some of them only loosely connected with those areas. It offers excellent practice for IELTS Listening Section 4. For many of the talks, you can listen with subtitles in English or in some other languages, and can read a transcript of the talk.

1 Unit 1, Listen 1

Examiner: Good morning. My name's Janet Miller. Can you tell me your full name, please?

Candidate: My name's Niran Boonmee.

Examiner: And can you tell me where you're from?

Candidate: I'm from Thailand.

Examiner: Can I see your identification, please?

***

Examiner: Thank you. In the first part, I'd like to ask you a few questions about yourself. What do you do? Do you work, or are you a student?

Candidate: Well, actually, both. I'm a part-time student. I'm doing a degree in Business Studies. I'm also working as a lifeguard at my local swimming pool.

Examiner: I see. What's the most interesting part of being a lifeguard?

Candidate: Well, to be honest, it's not a very interesting job. Most of the time we just wait by the pool. The most interesting part is probably the conversations I have with the other lifeguards. I've got to know them all pretty well, now.

Examiner: What's the most difficult part of being a lifeguard?

Candidate: We quite often have to tell children to stop behaving badly, and occasionally their parents get angry with us: 'Don't tell my children what to do!' – that kind of thing. That can be difficult.

Examiner: Would you say it's a good occupation?

Candidate: Well, yes and no. It's a very pleasant job in some ways, but as I said, it can be boring, and it's not very well paid. That's why I'm doing a degree. I want to get something better.

Examiner: I see. What are your career plans for the future?

Candidate: When I graduate, I want to get a job in a financial institution, maybe a bank or insurance company. I haven't decided exactly what yet, but something like that.

Examiner: OK. Now, let's talk about music. What kind of music do you like listening to?

Candidate: At the moment, I don't have a lot of time for listening to music, but my favourite type of music is …

 2 Unit 1, Listen 2

Examiner: In the first part, I'd like to ask you about the place where you live. Can you describe the building you live in?

Candidate: Yes, I live in an apartment block. It's got, I think, eight floors, and we're on the second floor. It's a modern block. I think it was built about 20 years ago.

Examiner: Is it similar to other buildings in the area?

Candidate: Yes, it is. There are lots of blocks very similar to mine in that part of the city.

Examiner: Is it in a convenient location for you?

Candidate: Hm, no, not really. It's quite far from the city centre. I'm studying at a college on the other side of the city, so I spend about two hours on the bus every day. It's quite boring. The bus is always quite crowded, and I often have to stand. Actually, it's probably the worst part of my day.

Examiner: I can imagine! Apart from the buses, do you like living in your city?

Candidate: Yes, I do. There's always a lot going on, and all my friends are there. It's very lively in the evenings. There are a lot of good bars and restaurants, and people come from all around the city to meet their friends and have a good time. It's a very good atmosphere.

Examiner: What changes would improve the area where you live?

Candidate: Like most cities, there's far too much traffic. I was talking about my bus journey every day. It's only about ten kilometres, but it takes so long because most of the time the bus is stuck in a traffic jam. Also, sometimes the city is quite polluted, especially when the weather's cold and there's no wind to blow away the pollution. So, less traffic and less pollution would be big improvements.

Examiner: OK. Now, let's talk about films and TV. What kinds of films and TV do you like watching?

Candidate: I don't go to the cinema very often. In fact, I haven't been for years. I don't watch a lot of TV, but when I do, I like to watch …

 3 Unit 2, Listen 1

Examiner: I'd like to ask you some questions about your free-time activities. What do you do at the weekends?

Candidate: Well, my final exams are next month, so at the moment I don't really have any free time at the weekends or any other days. However, in general, when I have free time, I like doing outdoor activities. In particular, I really like land-yachting.

Examiner: Land-yachting? What's that?

Candidate: Um, well, you have a little chariot with three wheels and a big sail. You sit on the chariot, and catch the wind in the sail to make the chariot move. There's a big, flat, windy beach quite near where I live, which is ideal for it. It's also called beach-yachting and also land-sailing. You don't have to do it on a beach. Any flat land will do.

Examiner: I see. What is it that you like about this sport?

Candidate: On a windy day, the chariots can go *really* fast, and because you're so close to the ground, you really feel the speed. It's a thrilling experience. To tell the truth, though, for every ten minutes you spend on the chariot, you probably spend an hour setting up the equipment and waiting for the wind to be right, but that's all part of the fun, too. It's great being outdoors, by the sea.

Examiner: How often do you get the chance to do it?

Candidate: In theory, you can do it all year round, but it's not a lot of fun in the freezing cold. It's mostly a summer sport. I suppose April to October are the main months. You also need wind, of course. Another factor is the other people on the beach. In July and August, the beach can get quite crowded, so at that time of year we mostly do it quite late in the day, when the beach is emptier. So generally I do it at the weekends from late spring to early autumn, but a bit less in the middle of the summer, for the reason I just said.

Examiner: How important a part of your week are your free-time activities?

Candidate: Actually, not really that important. Perhaps if I was working, my time off would be the most important part of the week in some ways, but because I'm a student, I don't so much feel the need to let my hair down at the weekends. I enjoy most of the time I'm studying, too. It's not like doing a stressful job.

Examiner: Do you enjoy your free time more now than you did when you were a child?

Candidate: Hm. That's a hard question to answer. I don't really remember how I felt about my free time when I was child. I used to go sand-yachting then, too. It was my father who got me started. I used to find it quite frightening, and now I don't, so in that respect, I suppose I enjoy my free time more now.

Examiner: What free-time activity would you like to try in the future?

Candidate: I'd love to try real sailing. You know, with a boat on the sea or a lake. I've never done it. I imagine it's probably a bit more difficult than sand-yachting.

🎧 ④ Unit 2, Listen 2

Examiner: Now, let's talk about books and magazines. What kind of books and magazines do you like reading?

Candidate: Um, I'm really not bothered about magazines. I never buy them, and I hardly ever read them – only if I'm in the dentist's waiting room, or somewhere else where there's nothing better to read. I don't really have an opinion about them.

Examiner: I see. So what sort of books do you like?

Candidate: I don't read many novels. I'm much more interested in non-fiction. I'm a big fan of biographies. I think there's a lot to be learned from the lives of famous people. I like reference books. Obviously you can't sit down and read an atlas or a dictionary of quotations, but I often spend time looking through that kind of book. Again, there's a lot to be learned from them.

Examiner: Do you like reading any other types of book?

Candidate: Well, as I said, I don't read many novels. I quite like crime fiction. At the moment, I'm reading a book by Michael Dibden about an Italian detective called Aurelio Zen. It's quite good.

Examiner: Have the types of book you like changed over the years?

Candidate: Sorry, I didn't catch that. Could you repeat the question?

Examiner: Have the types of book you like changed over the years?

Candidate: No, not really. Obviously my tastes now are different to my tastes as a child, but apart from that, I don't think they've really changed at all.

Examiner: Do you prefer reading books or newspapers?

Candidate: Ah, well, I'm obsessed with news and current affairs. I buy two newspapers every day and I read both of them. I spend much more time reading newspapers than books, so I suppose that must mean I prefer them.

🎧 ⑤ Unit 3, Listen 1

Examiner: I'm going to give you a topic, and I'd like you to talk about it for one to two minutes. Before you talk, you have one minute to think about what you're going to say. You can make some notes if you wish. Here's a pencil and some paper for making notes.

Candidate: Thanks.

Examiner: Here's your topic on this task card. I'd like you to describe the job or career you have or hope to have in the future.

Candidate: OK, thank you.

***

Examiner: Now, remember that you have one to two minutes for this. Don't worry if I stop you. I'll tell you when the time is up. Can you start speaking now, please?

Candidate: Right, OK ... I'm going to talk about my job as a waiter. It's not a very difficult job, of course, but it's more complicated than most people think. The customers are spending a lot of money, and they expect to have a perfect evening. You have to, er, you have to be kind of an actor, playing the role of the perfect waiter. It can be hard to do that at the end of a long evening when you're tired, but I try my best! Most of the customers seem nice people. I enjoy meeting them, and I want to do the best I can to help them have a good time when they come to the restaurant.

So, why did I choose to become a waiter? Well, actually, I didn't really choose it. A couple of years ago, I had just finished college and didn't have a job. A friend of mine was working in the restaurant and somebody was off sick, so I went to help out for a few days. Then I just ... stayed. I started to like it. The basic pay is very low, but I earn quite a lot in tips, so in fact it's quite well paid. The best part is that I have a lot of fun with the other people who work there. We're all really good friends. The only part of the job I really don't like is the hours. I can never go out on a Friday or Saturday night because I'm always at work. However, I'm not going to do this job for the rest of my life. I've been applying for other jobs recently.

Examiner: What sort of jobs have you been applying for?

Candidate: My degree is in Media Studies, and so I'd really like to work in the media in some form. So I've been applying to local radio stations and a local TV production company. They don't have any vacancies at the moment, but I keep reminding them who I am. I'm going to apply to some other companies related to the media as well.

🎧 ⑥ Unit 3, Listen 2

Examiner: Good luck with that. Can I have the task card back, please? Thanks. We've been talking about jobs. I'd like to discuss with you one or two more general questions relating to this. Let's consider the balance between work and free time. Do you think that the balance between work and free time in your country is about right?

Candidate: Ah … I think it depends. For example, people who have government jobs mostly only work around 37, maybe 40 hours a week. However, in my country a lot of people have their own small businesses. Really, a lot of people. And if you have a shop, for example, it can be difficult to decide to close. You don't know if another customer is just about to come through the door with a lot of money to spend. From what I've seen, people with their own shops regularly work extremely long hours, up to perhaps 14 hours a day, seven days a week. The same can be true for other people who work for themselves.

Examiner: I see. And what problems can be caused by too much work, do you think?

Candidate: It … it can cause problems for family life, in my opinion. It's obviously not very good for children if they hardly ever see their parents. And from what I've seen, it can be very bad for relationships between married couples if they just work continuously and never have any fun together. I'm sure this is a common reason for divorces.

Examiner: What can people do if they feel they are expected to do too much work?

Candidate: Well, there's a law in my country which limits the working week to … I think it's 48 hours per week, maybe even less. But bosses frequently take no notice of this, so it can be a problem. If somebody is asked to work more than this, they should speak to their boss and ask to be given less work. But of course this can be difficult. It's not always easy to make a complaint to your boss. From what I've seen, they tend to make employees feel guilty for complaining.

Examiner: Mm. Now let's consider workaholics. Why do you think some people work so much that they become workaholics?

Candidate: Workaholics? Obviously it depends on the person, but in my experience, it's … well, it's not really the money that makes them workaholics. I think it's just something in their personalities which doesn't allow them to … mm, to stop thinking about work and switch off. For example, I have a friend who runs his own website. He works on it all the time. I don't think he sleeps much! But he doesn't make a lot of money from it – just enough to live. And I don't think he would make less money if he worked on it less. He's become a perfectionist. Every part of the site has to be absolutely perfect. It's become a kind of obsession for him. I think he's happy, but he just doesn't really have any interests at all apart from his work. I guess that's just how he likes to live his life. It's up to him!

Examiner: Thank you very much. That's the end of the Speaking test.

 **7** **Unit 4, Listen 1**

Examiner: I'm going to give you a topic, and I'd like you to talk about it for one to two minutes. Before you talk, you have one minute to think about what you're going to say. You can make some notes if you wish. Here's a pencil and some paper for making notes.

Candidate: Thank you.

Examiner: Here's your topic on this task card. I'd like you to describe a teacher who influenced you.

Candidate: OK, thank you.

***

Examiner: Now, remember that you have one to two minutes for this. Don't worry if I stop you. I'll tell you when the time is up. Can you start speaking now, please?

Candidate: I'm going to talk about a teacher I had at primary school. This was when I was about ten years old. He was a drama teacher, but he wasn't a permanent teacher at the school, and he didn't come every day. I think he visited just one day a week, and the other days he worked in other schools in the area. Well, I suppose he did. I never asked him about it. Anyway, I was quite a shy kid. I didn't have many friends, and I wasn't very confident about most things. We started drama classes when I was ten, and I absolutely loved it. Instead of being shy, I was much more confident, and I found I could make the other kids laugh. This drama teacher noticed that I was good at acting, and he encouraged me to take the lead role in the school play that year. At first, I didn't want to, because I felt too scared to perform in front of the whole school, but he more or less forced me to take the role. And he was right to do that, because I was a big success in the play, and then instead of being a bit of a nobody in the school, everybody knew who I was, I had many more friends and I became less shy. I did some more acting afterwards at secondary school, but after a while I lost interest in it. The way that drama teacher influenced me was by helping me to increase my confidence and making me believe in myself more. I'm sure that helped me in later years.

Examiner: Would you like to meet this teacher again now?

Candidate: Well, he was pretty old then, probably just before retirement. I hope he's still alive. If he is, I'd like to thank him for forcing me to believe in myself and take that part in the play.

 8 **Unit 4, Listen 2**

Examiner: Can I have the task card back, please? Thank you. We've been talking about teachers and schools. I'd like to discuss with you one or two more general questions relating to this. Let's talk about the schools in your country. Do many of them have problems with children behaving badly in lessons?

Candidate: Well, I don't know much about what happens in schools today, but a few years ago, when I was at school, I'd say, yes, there was a problem with some students behaving badly. It wasn't in all lessons, but in some lessons a lot of time was wasted with the teacher trying to get everybody to stop talking or sending messages on their mobile phones, and start working.

Examiner: Why do you think some children behave badly in lessons?

Candidate: Hm. That's a good question. I think there are two reasons. Partly, I think it's because some of the children don't have enough respect for the teacher. Perhaps this is something their parents should have taught them. However, I think the main reason is often that the lessons aren't interesting enough. If the students don't respect the teacher, you have to ask *why* they don't respect him or her. In my experience, the teachers who gave interesting lessons didn't usually have many problems with discipline.

Examiner: In your country, do you think most pupils find the school subjects interesting?

Candidate: Well, again, I think there are two points to make here. One is that it depends on the students – for example, some kids find maths fascinating, others find it really boring. The other point, though, is that it can depend on the teacher. A good teacher can make a boring subject interesting, and vice versa. It's up to the teacher to make the pupils interested in the subject.

Examiner: Have schools in your country changed since you were at school?

Candidate: I haven't really thought about that. As I said, I don't know much about schools today. I imagine they've changed in some ways. For example … well, when I was at school, quite a lot of students had mobile phones with them all the time, but now I expect almost all of them do. Or perhaps none of them does – I think I heard that mobile phones have been completely banned in some schools. I expect there are more computers now, too. At my primary school, there were about 200 children and one computer room with about ten computers. I'm sure there are more than that now.

Examiner: Do you think children today are different to children when you were young?

Candidate: Well, I do know something about this. My sister has twins aged 11. I meet them and their friends quite often, and they seem a bit different to the 11-year-olds I remember. Although they're very similar in many ways, they seem a little bit more confident and they also seem to know more about the news and current affairs. When I was 11, I don't think I knew much at all about the news, but they seem to know quite a lot. More than I do, sometimes!

Examiner: Thank you very much. That's the end of the Speaking test.

 9 **Unit 5, Listen 1**

Examiner: I'm going to give you a topic, and I'd like you to talk about it for one to two minutes. Before you talk, you have one minute to think about what you're going to say. You can make some notes if you wish. Here's a pencil and some paper for making notes.

Candidate: Thanks.

Examiner: Here's your topic on this task card. I'd like you to describe a city you have visited.

Candidate: OK, thank you.

***

Examiner: Now, remember that you have one to two minutes for this. Don't worry if I stop you. I'll tell you when the time is up. Can you start speaking now, please?

Candidate: I don't have a lot of experience of visiting other cities. I live in Rome, which of course is a very big city, and when I go on vacation with my family, we prefer to get away from the city and go to the beach or visit the countryside. So I'm going to talk about a very small city in the south of Italy called Lecce. It seems more like a town, really, but technically it's a city because it's the administrative capital of the region. I don't think it's well known outside Italy. I went there because two years ago, my

family had a beach holiday about 20 kilometres away, and we went into Lecce to go to restaurants there. I remember it well, because we went there five or six times.

When you drive through the outskirts, it really doesn't appear to be a very interesting place. I'm not saying it's unpleasant, but there are lots of very ordinary apartment blocks and a lot of traffic congestion. However, when you actually get to the centre and find somewhere to park, it's very nice. There are several beautiful old churches, and the historic centre is surprisingly pleasant. Most of the shops seem quite old-fashioned – some of them give the impression that nothing has changed since the 1950s. The whole place feels very relaxed, and the local people are extremely friendly. You get the feeling that they're happy living there, and are proud of their city. I liked it very much.

Examiner: Would you like to live there?

Candidate: Yes, I would. I think I'd be very happy there.

Examiner: Do you think you will visit Lecce again?

Candidate: I'd like to. Perhaps we'll have another summer holiday in that area some time soon.

Examiner: It sounds a nice place.

 10 **Unit 5, Listen 2**

Examiner: Now, can I have the task card back, please? Thank you. We've been talking about towns and cities. I'd like to discuss with you one or two more general questions relating to this. Let's talk about living in cities and the countryside. Do you think life is better in the city or in the countryside?

Candidate: I suppose it depends on the person. In many ways, life is easier in the countryside. By that I mean that there's more space, no crowds and it's usually cheaper to live. On the other hand, it can be a lot less interesting. Most cultural activity goes on in cities. Personally, I wouldn't want to live outside a city, but I've lived in Rome all my life. I imagine that if I'd lived all my life in a small village, I probably wouldn't want to live in a city.

Examiner: In many countries, cities are growing fast. Why do you think this is?

Candidate: Um, I'm not sure. Perhaps it's because in some countries, the standard of living in the countryside is very low, and life for a lot of people is just about growing enough food to live. I guess many people in that situation (a) get bored and (b) hope to find a higher standard of living in the city.

Examiner: What problems can rapidly expanding cities have?

Candidate: Let me think. Um … well, when cities expand very rapidly, it's often without any control over how they develop. In other words, they become megacities with huge shanty-towns and no proper – what's the word – infrastructure for millions of people. Unfortunately, a lot of people don't find the better life they were hoping for, and can end up in an even worse situation. This is probably one of the biggest problems we face today.

Examiner: Some cities receive millions of visitors. What problems can this cause?

Candidate: Ah, well, this is an entirely different problem, and I know a lot more about this because I live in Rome. If you go into the historic centre on a Saturday in the summer, it can seem that you're the only local inhabitant there. The problem is that cities with too many visitors can lose their original character. Although of course it's not a problem for people who own restaurants and shops in the historic centre. To put it another way, tourism supports a lot of people financially.

Examiner: What can be done to ensure tourism doesn't cause too many problems?

Candidate: That's not an easy question to answer. If you limit tourist numbers, you also limit the benefits to the local economy. And how do you limit visitor numbers? You can't put a wall around a city. If the tourist board in my city tried harder to promote the less-famous parts of the city, the visitors might spread out. There are some beautiful areas outside the centre, with some great historic monuments, but very few tourists go there because they're all in the most famous places in the centre.

Examiner: Thank you very much. That's the end of the Speaking test.

 11 Unit 6, Listen 1

Examiner: Can you start speaking now, please?

Candidate: One of my favourite TV shows for a long time has been *The Simpsons*. It's very famous, but I'll describe it anyway. It's a cartoon sitcom about an ordinary family in an ordinary town in the USA. There's a large cast of other characters, and sometimes famous people play themselves. It's been running for more than 20 years, and it's one of the most popular TV programmes in the world.
I sometimes watch it on regular TV, which is dubbed. At the moment, it's on Sunday evenings. I don't enjoy that so much, partly because I think the dubbed version isn't quite as funny as the original version and partly because they only show old episodes, and I've seen most of them before. Last year, we got satellite TV and we get a channel which shows the original English version. I much prefer that. It's quite fast, and I find it quite difficult to follow, but I usually watch it with subtitles in English, which helps. I sometimes record it and watch it again, and the second time I can usually understand it a lot more easily.
The reason I like it is simple. It makes me laugh. The humour is very fast, and it seems a little more sophisticated than most sitcoms. There are lots of little extra jokes which are easy to miss, but which you notice the second time you watch it. Some people say it isn't as funny as it used to be, but I disagree. I think it's as good as it's ever been.

Examiner: How much TV do you watch?

Candidate: It depends. In the winter, I watch quite a lot, maybe 15, 20 hours a week. But in the summer, I watch a lot less. I prefer to be outside with my family or friends.

 12 Unit 6, Listen 2

Examiner: We've been talking about television. I'd like to discuss with you one or two more general questions relating to this. Let's talk about the news on TV and from other sources. How important do you think it is to keep up to date with news and current events?

Candidate: I think it's very important to know what's happening in your country and in the world. Having said that, I don't actually follow the news carefully every day. I think it's essential to keep up to date with major events, but I don't think it's necessary to follow the details of every news story. At least, it isn't for me. I just follow the main stories.

Examiner: In your opinion, what's the best source of news: TV, newspapers, the Internet or something else?

Candidate: Well, I mostly watch the news on TV, but I think newspapers are probably the best source. They go into much more detail than TV news, and there's more variety. They cover a much wider range of stories. I'm not sure about the Internet for news. It's very convenient to be able to check the news any time you want, but I'm not sure that all news sites are very good quality. On some of them, there seem to be a lot of stories about celebrities, and not so much about serious topics and events.

Examiner: Let's talk about other types of reporting now. Documentary films for the cinema seldom attract large audiences. Why do you think this is?

Candidate: I suppose they're just not as entertaining as fictional films. They may be exciting for people who have a special interest in the subject, but apart from that, they tend not to have a lot of appeal. On the other hand, a good fictional film can be entertaining for almost everybody. When people go to the cinema, mostly they want to be entertained rather than educated.

Examiner: Some people feel there should be more serious documentaries and dramas on TV and in the cinema. Do you agree or disagree with this?

Candidate: Hmm. I don't really know if I agree or disagree. Of course, it would be good to see more serious TV programmes and films, but I'm not sure it's a good idea to try to control what kind of things get made. TV companies and film producers make what they think people want to see. I can't imagine them making things people don't want to see, just because somebody tells them to.

Examiner: What do you think could be done to promote more serious types of TV programme and cinema film?

Candidate: In my country, we have one arts channel which is owned by the government. It shows documentaries and films that probably wouldn't get shown on more popular channels. I think film festivals are a good idea, too. They generate a lot of interest in smaller films and independent producers. Many of those films are documentaries and serious dramas.

 13 Unit 7, Listen 1

Examiner: Can you start speaking now, please?

Candidate: Most summers when I was a child, my family went to the same campsite in a family holiday resort, an old fishing village called Puertonuevo, on the coast a couple of hours by car from our home. It wasn't a remarkable place. The beach, which was really big and sandy, I liked very much, but the town itself wasn't beautiful or interesting, and I don't remember there being anything much there apart from a few hotels, restaurants and self-catering apartments. But I loved those holidays. Usually, my parents were quite strict, but on holiday my sister and I were allowed to do more or less whatever we liked. We had so much fun! Whenever it was sunny, my parents liked to lie on the beach working on their suntans, and my sister, who's two years younger than me, and I used to make sandcastles, explore rock pools and play with other kids who were there. In the evenings, we went back to the campsite, which had a wonderful view out over the sea, and usually had a big barbecue in front of the tent. I have very happy memories of those holidays, and whenever I visit a small beach resort, I remember those times.

Examiner: Would you like to visit this place again?

Candidate: Yes, I would. I haven't been back since the last of those holidays, which was when I was about 15. It would be great to see the place again and find out if it's changed much.

Examiner: What kind of visitor do you think this place suits best?

Candidate: I think it's perfect for families with children who just want a pleasant, relaxing beach holiday, and who don't want to spend a lot of money.

 **14** Unit 7, Listen 2

Examiner: We've been talking about holidays. I'd like to discuss with you one or two more general questions relating to this. Let's talk about travel and tourism in general. Millions of Western tourists visit holiday resorts in developing countries. What do you think attracts them?

Candidate: Well, price is probably a major factor. It tends to be cheaper to visit developing countries. For many Western tourists, though, perhaps it's more because they want to have an experience which is really different from their normal lives. They feel they will be able to get that by visiting what seems to them an exotic country far away.

Examiner: What difficulties can Western visitors experience in developing countries?

Candidate: Things that they take for granted back home, such as clean water, good roads and electricity that's always on, may not be available. Another very common problem is getting ill, especially from eating food which has been washed in unclean water. A friend of mine went to India recently. She told me she was there for a month and spent the entire time feeling sick! A third problem is that some areas may be dangerous. Obviously, there are problems with violent crime in almost all countries, but in a very different culture it can be difficult to judge what kind of situation is potentially dangerous.

Examiner: How can large numbers of Western visitors affect the lives of ordinary people in developing countries?

Candidate: The obvious benefit is that tourism can create jobs and provide money for the local economy, which can then be spent on improving schools, hospitals, etc. The downside is that rich foreign tourists who don't know what things normally cost can cause prices to rise for local people. If you're a pineapple seller, for example, and tourists will buy your pineapples for five dollars, then why sell them to local people for one dollar?

Examiner: What do you understand by the phrase *responsible tourism?*

Candidate: Responsible tourism ... I think that means being aware of the effects of tourism on local people. It means you should behave in a way which benefits the local culture, or at least doesn't harm it.

Examiner: What can visitors do to ensure they are responsible tourists?

Candidate: Obviously, it's important to do some research before you go, so you know about local problems, like water shortages, for example. Then when you arrive, it's a good idea to try to spend money with local businesses. For example, eat in locally owned restaurants rather than international chains, that sort of thing. It's also important to respect local customs and behave in a civilized way. Just because you're a long way from home, it doesn't mean you can behave however you like and do whatever you want, regardless of the feelings of local people.

15 Unit 8, Predicting and practising 1, Exercise 2

Woman 1: What's your name, please?

Man 1: Gérard Ozeville.

Woman 1: How do you spell that?

Man 1: First name, G-E-R-A-R-D. Surname, Ozeville, O-Z-E-V-I-double L-E.

Woman 1: Thank you, and can I have your address, please?

Man 1: Sure. It's 16A, Aston Street ...

Woman 1: How do you spell that?

Man 1: A-S-T-O-N.

Woman 1: Thanks.

Man 1: Ilfracombe, that's I-L-F-R-A-C-O-M-B-E, postcode EX34 9GW.

Woman 1: And your telephone number?

Man 1: It's 01272 863990.

***

Woman 1: Can I take your credit-card number, please?

Man 1: It's 4893 9607 6220 4554.

Woman 1: Thanks. And the expiry date?

Man 1: It's 11/19.

Woman 1: Thank you very much.

***

Man 1: Can you confirm my booking, please?

Woman 1: No problem. Here it is. Check in the 16th of July, check out the 21st of July, one standard double room.

Man 1: Thank you very much.

***

Man 2: Hello, what are the prices for next Saturday evening?

Woman 2: It's 42 euros for the front rows of the stalls, that's rows A to H, and all other stalls seats are 29.50. Circle seats are all 34.50.

Man 2: Thanks. And what time does it start?

Woman 2: Half past seven.

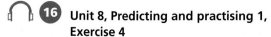

16 Unit 8, Predicting and practising 1, Exercise 4

Narrator: You will hear a woman phoning a hospital to ask about a job vacancy advertised in the local newspaper.

Woman 1: Good morning. Englefield Hospital Human Resources Department. My name's Dawn. How can I help you?

Woman 2: Hello, I'm calling about the job advertised in yesterday's *Evening News*.

Woman 1: Um, we have several jobs advertised at the moment. Which one are you calling about?

Woman 2: X-ray Department Receptionist.

Woman 1: Oh yes, I remember that vacancy. Right, can I just take some details first? Starting with your name, please?

Woman 2: Jill Adderstone.

Woman 1: OK, is that Jill with a J?

Woman 2: Yes, it is.

Woman 1: And how do you spell your surname, please?

Woman 2: It's A-double D-E-R-S-T-O-N-E.

Woman 1: OK. Thank you. And can I take your address, please?

Woman 2: Sure. It's number 1-4-7, Bonham Street.

Woman 1: Is that B-O-N-H-A-M?

Woman 2: That's correct, and the city is Leicester.

Woman 1: And can I take your postcode too, please?

Woman 2: Of course. It's LE2 6HV.

Woman 1: Right. And just one more thing for the computer – can I take your phone number, please?

Woman 2: I've just moved there, and I only have a mobile at the moment. Is that OK?

Woman 1: That's no problem at all.

Woman 2: Right, it's ... let me think, I keep forgetting it ... OK, it's 07488 269010.

Woman 1: Can I ask, do you have any previous experience of reception work?

Woman 2: Yes, I do. I've been a receptionist at the Imperial Hotel for the last 13 years, but it's closing down next month, unfortunately.

Woman 1: I see. I'm sorry to hear that. There's just one more question I need to ask you. When would you be available to start?

Woman 2: Um, just a moment while I look at my diary. OK ... I could start from Monday the 11th of June.

Woman 1: That sounds fine. Well, we're interviewing Wednesday and Thursday next week. Is there any particular time you can't manage then?

Woman 2: Um, well, I can't do Wednesday, I'm afraid, as I'll be at work, but Thursday's one of my days off, so any time then would be OK.

Woman 1: 10.30 a.m.?

Woman 2: That's fine.

Woman 1: And you know where we are?

Woman 2: Yes, I do. The address is in the advertisement ... but do you mind if I ask a couple of questions about the job? I'll have to travel quite a long way, and I want to be sure it's the kind of job I'm looking for.

Woman 1: OK, that sounds reasonable. What do you want to know?

17 Unit 8, Predicting and practising 2, Exercise 2

1

Woman: So all my possessions will be covered, is that right?

Man: No, not exactly. It covers all possessions except bicycles and cameras. You'd have to get a separate policy for each of those.

2

Woman: So what type of accommodation are you looking for, exactly?

Man: A one-bedroom flat. It's just for me, so I don't need anything larger.

3

Man: So now we just need to choose the restaurant.

Woman: Well, ideally we want somewhere that's not too expensive and a type of food that everyone likes, but the most important thing is that it's near the office. We'll be walking there and back, and we don't know what the weather will be like.

18 Unit 8, Predicting and practising 2, Exercise 3

Narrator: You will hear a conversation in a school between a teacher and a parent of one of the pupils.

Woman: Hello, excuse me, do you have a moment?

Man: Yes, of course. How can I help?

Woman: I wondered if you could answer a few questions I have about the school trip next week. I think all the children were given a letter about it to give to their parents, but I'm afraid my son Ian lost his on the way home. I don't even know where he's going!

Man: Oh, yes, you're Mrs ... Mrs Ogilvy, is that right?

Woman: Yes, I am.

Man: I don't teach Ian myself, but I know who he is. He's doing very well in the school football team! Anyway, the trip's to Whitsmead Wildlife Park.

Woman: Oh yes, I know it. It's very nice.

Man: The coach leaves at 8 a.m.

Woman: Where does it leave from? Outside the school?

Man: No, not exactly. The road's too narrow there for coaches. It's leaving from the public car park.

Woman: The one next to the school?

Man: That's right.

Woman: Will my son need to take a packed lunch?

Man: Yes, he will.

Woman: And anything else?

Man: Um, no, that's all, I think. There's just one other thing. We're still waiting to hear from the coach company how long the journey's going to take, so we'll be phoning all the parents in a day or two to tell them the exact return time. But it'll be some time between five and six, probably.

Woman: I see, that's fine. But I'd better give the secretary my new contact details. We've just moved.

Man: I'll make a note of them right now if you like, and pass them to the secretary later. Would that be easier?

Woman: Yes, that's very kind of you.

Man: I'll just get a pen. Bear with me for a moment ...

Narrator: You will hear a number of different recordings, and you will have to answer questions on what you hear. There will be time for you to read the instructions and the questions, and you will have a chance to check your work. All the recordings will be played once only. The test is in four sections. At the end of the real test, you will be given ten minutes to transfer your answers to an answer sheet.

Section 1

You will hear two people discussing travel arrangements from an airport to a city centre. First, you have some time to look at Questions 1 to 5. You will see that there is an example which has been done for you. On this occasion only, the conversation relating to this will be played first.

Man 1: So, the flight lands at just after half past eleven in the evening. How are we going to get to the city centre?

Man 2: I've got the airport website here on my phone. Let's have a look and see what the options are. I just need to find the right page ... er, yes, here we are.

Man 1: What does it say?

Man 2: Um ... there's a shuttle train. They go every half hour and it takes 12 minutes. Mm, that's quick!

Narrator: The train journey takes 12 minutes, so the answer *12 minutes* has been written into the table. Now we will begin. You should answer the questions as you listen because you will not hear the recording a second time. Listen carefully and answer Questions 1 to 5.

Man 1: So, the flight lands at just after half past eleven in the evening. How are we going to get to the city centre?

Man 2: I've got the airport website here on my phone. Let's have a look and see what the options are. I just need to find the right page ... er, yes, here we are.

Man 1: What does it say?

Man 2: Um ... there's a shuttle train. They go every half hour and it takes 12 minutes. Mm, that's quick!

Man 1: Not bad. How much does it cost?

Man 2: It's 15 dollars.

Man 1: That sounds OK.

Man 2: Ah, but unfortunately they only run from 5 a.m. to a quarter to midnight, so that's no good. We'll be arriving just too late for the last one. Never mind. There's a 24-hour bus service. They go at 20 minutes past the hour, so if we miss the 12.20, we could get the 1.20.

Man 1: How much is it?

Man 2: It's only 11 dollars, but it takes 45 minutes. Hmm. That's quite slow, and it's a long wait if we miss the 12.20.

Man 1: What about a taxi?

Man 2: It says here a taxi takes about 20 minutes. It doesn't give the cost, though.

Man 1: It'll probably only be a bit more expensive than two bus tickets, and we won't have to wait.

Man 2: The website gives a link to an airport taxi company. Let's have a look ... Yes, it's got all the information here. It costs 38 dollars, and it's also a 24-hour service.

Man 1: I think that's OK.

Man 2: It's not a lot more expensive than the bus for two of us, and much more convenient. They take advance reservations, too.

Man 1: I think we should book it, then. Arriving at that time of night, we don't want to find that there aren't any taxis there.

Man 2: I agree. Shall I read out the details, and you write them down?

Man 1: OK. What does it say?

Narrator: Before you hear the rest of the conversation, you have some time to look at Questions 6 to 10. Now listen and answer Questions 6 to 10.

Man 2: Normally, you go to their office in the arrivals hall in the airport, but after 10 p.m., the office is closed.

Man 1: Oh. Does it say what you have to do if you arrive later than that?

Man 2: Yes. You have to call them when your plane lands.

Man 1: That's OK, our mobile phones will work there.

Man 2: You give them a call when your plane lands, and then the taxi will be waiting for you outside the arrivals hall, by a sign that says 'Airport Taxi Service'. You have to pay the driver in cash, so we'll need some dollars.

Man 1: Do you know if there's a cash machine at the airport?

Man 2: Yes, there is – I used it last time I was there.

Man 1: So that's no problem. Is there an online booking form?

Man 2: Um ... no. To make a reservation, we have to phone the office between 7 a.m. and 10 p.m. Or we can book by sending them an email. We just email them our details, and then they'll send us a booking reference number which we have to show to the driver. That's all.

Man 1: OK, let's do it by email, then. It'll be easier than phoning. What's their email address?

Man 2: It's info at ercancars.com. That's info at E-R-C-A-N-C-A-R-S dot com. Got that?

Man 1: Yes.

Man 2: Good. I'll open up the email on my phone and send them one right now.

Thank you for coming to this introductory talk. Firstly, I'd like to welcome you all to Beachwood Holiday Village – or welcome you back if you've stayed here before, of course. Well, first things first. Sorry to start with this, but we've seen quite a few cars parked on the road leading to the town today. Please note that guests should park their cars in the designated area by the main entrance. At busy times, that can become very full, and for when this happens, there's an overspill parking area to one side of the village, on the far side of the pool. There are always plenty of spaces there, and it's just by the river, so you won't get lost! We ask you not to leave your cars on the road because local residents use it to park on, and if they can't find a space, we get some angry phone calls! So thank you in advance for your understanding about this.

Now, as I'm sure you're all aware, the village is divided into two zones. The larger zone, at the front of the complex where we are now, is the family zone. The children's play area is here, between the main car park and Sandcastles restaurant, where we're sitting now. Of course, everybody is welcome in this part. Then on the other side of the river, we have the adults-only zone. I expect those of you who've checked into this part are hoping for a peaceful holiday, so those of you with kids – please do try to make sure they understand that they shouldn't cross the river. Down the far end of the adult zone is another restaurant and attached bar. As you'd expect, that's also for adults only, but it's open at lunchtime, so those of you with kids taking part in our Kid's Club activities don't need to miss out. You can get yourself an excellent lunch there while we're entertaining your youngsters. Now, the path running alongside the river – that leads down to the beach, as I expect you've all discovered already. And of course our lovely barbecue area is down there, on the sand. Oh, one last thing – I hope you all remembered to bring everything you need, but if there's anything you've forgotten, you may well find it for sale in our mini-market. It's easy to find, right next to this restaurant, and just a few steps from the swimming pool. You can't miss it!

 21 Unit 8, Preparing to answer 2, Exercise 3

Narrator: You will hear a speaker talking to a group of local people who have come to hear about the arrangements for a boat show. First you have some time to look at Questions 11 to 15.
Listen carefully to the first part of the talk, and answer Questions 11 to 15.

Speaker: Good afternoon. Thanks to you all for attending this planning meeting for this year's boat show. As you all know, it's the biggest boat show in the country, and this time we're expecting more visitors than ever before. So we need to make sure everything is properly planned and runs as smoothly as possible.
Let's look first at the plan of the main show area. Does everybody have that? Good. Those of you who have been involved with previous boat shows here will notice that we've made some major changes. Instead of having several entrances, we've decided to have just one large one for visitors, and a small service entrance off to one side for exhibitors and technical personnel. This means that if you're a visitor, the first thing you'll see when you enter is a digital information board showing the events of the day. Beyond that are some steps, and you go down these to the main display area, passing the first-aid tent on your left and then the main snacks and refreshments area on the right. Last year's catering wasn't a great success, to be honest. It made very little money for the show, and we're hoping to do much better this year, with a much wider range of products. And on the

subject of spending money, we're also going to install a couple of cashpoints just behind the refreshments area. We don't want people running out of cash while they're here! Anyway, going back to the main route through the show ground, the steps lead down to the exhibition area. Now, before you reach the boats, you're going to see the stands of the smaller companies who make sails, navigation equipment, nautical paint ... that kind of thing. The suppliers, in other words, rather than the boat-builders. We've arranged it like this because last year, the companies with those stands complained that very few people visited them. This year, you'll have to go right past their stands in order to get to what most people will have come to see – all the very latest boat designs. So there you have it. Quite a different layout to last year.

Narrator: Before you hear the rest of the talk, you have some time to look at Questions 16 to 20.
Now listen, and answer Questions 16 to 20.

Speaker: We've also made some changes to the ticketing arrangements. This year, we've started selling tickets six months in advance instead of three, and have already sold a lot, although this may be because we're actually reducing the cost of tickets this year. That's right, you heard correctly. We've cut the cost of normal tickets. We're also selling e-tickets online again this year, despite the technical problems we had last time. Then, they were a little cheaper than paper tickets. The price of the online tickets remains unchanged, and they now cost the same as a paper ticket. Why are we reducing prices when everybody else is raising them? A criticism in the past has been that tickets are too expensive, and we want to make the show affordable for everybody. To compensate, we're raising the fees slightly for the exhibitors' stands, and we'll also add a bit to the price of the brochures. They sold extremely well last year, and nobody seemed to think they were too expensive. Another big change, as I've no doubt you're all aware, is that we've extended the show by two days. As well as increasing ticket sales, we're hoping this will help to ease some of the problems we've had in recent years with traffic congestion in the surrounding area. Connected with that, we're also hoping to encourage more local people to leave their cars at home by halving the price of the special shuttle bus from the city centre.
Those are all the main points, I think. Are there any questions so far?

 22 Unit 9, Focus on formats 1, Exercise 3

Tutor: I understand why you want to do 'Twentieth-century American novels', but the problem is that the seminars coincide with the seminars for 'Nineteenth-century poetry', and you said you wanted to do that, too.

Student: What if I did 'Medieval Poetry' and 'Twentieth-century American novels'? That's possible on the timetable.

Tutor: Well, yes, it is, but all your other courses have focused on the 18th century and later. If you do a course on the medieval period now, it won't fit very well with the other things you've studied, will it? This is your final year, so you won't have time to do any other medieval courses.

Student: That's true. I do want to do some poetry, though. I haven't done any yet. Only novels and plays.

Tutor: The only other poetry course next semester is 'Contemporary poetry'.

Student: Well, as I said, I've done several courses on the novel, and 'Contemporary poetry' would go very well with 'Nineteenth-century poetry', wouldn't it? It would be interesting to compare poetry from the two different periods.

Tutor: That means you won't be able to do 'Twentieth-century American novels'. The course won't be running again this academic year.

Student: I can live without it. I did 'Contemporary American novels' last semester, anyway.

Tutor: OK. That's fine by me, then.

🎧 **23**   **Unit 9, Preparing to answer 1, Exercise 2**

Narrator: Alex is a student at university. He has handed an essay to his tutor. The tutor has read it, and now they are discussing ways the next essay he writes can be improved. First, you have some time to look at Questions 21 to 25.
Listen carefully to the first part of the conversation, and answer Questions 21 to 25.

Tutor: Hello, Alex.

Alex: Hi.

Tutor: Well, I was impressed by your essay. It's certainly an improvement on the previous one.

Alex: That's good news. I worked on it for a long time, and I remembered the things you told me to do in our last tutorial.

Tutor: I can see that you did. You've addressed most of the problems I pointed out last time. In particular, you make points clearly and then support them with evidence, as we discussed.

Alex: So that aspect is all right?

Tutor: Definitely. But you could still do some work on the structure. All the points are good and well supported, but I didn't really sense an argument developing. It seems more a list of points.

Alex: OK, I see. As you suggested, I read some other essays, and tried to use a similar technique for the structure. I thought I structured my arguments better this time, too. I was quite pleased with the results.

Tutor: Well, it's an improvement on your previous work, and this is still only the first term. I'm not expecting perfection at this stage. And there are one or two other small things you could look at. You still give your opinions in a way which is too personal. It's OK to say what you think, but it should be a supported argument, not just a sentence beginning with 'In my opinion'. You did that three or four times.

Alex: So I shouldn't do that?

Tutor: No, not in formal academic writing. You should always write in a more impersonal style than that.

Alex: OK. I see.

Tutor: And there was one other thing ... ah, what was it?

... Oh yes, the length of the paragraphs. They're too long. In the second paragraph, for example, you make two main points, and it should be two shorter paragraphs.

Alex: OK, yes, I can see now that should be two paragraphs. I'll be more careful about that next time.

Tutor: Good. It's not a difficult thing, really. I'm sure you'll get the hang of it soon enough.

Alex: Is there a maximum number of words for one paragraph?

Tutor: Hm ... interesting question. Not really. But each paragraph should have one clear aim. In some academic books, paragraphs occasionally go on for several pages, but the writer will usually be making one main point.

Alex: Yes, I've read some like that. Shorter paragraphs are certainly easier to follow.

Tutor: Yes, indeed, and in undergraduate essays, unless there's a very good reason, a paragraph shouldn't normally be longer than three or four hundred words. If you find one has come out much longer than that, see if you can find a way to divide it into two.

Alex: OK, I understand. I'll remember that for next time.

Narrator: Before you hear the rest of the conversation, you have some time to look at Questions 26 to 30. Now listen, and answer Questions 26 to 30.

Tutor: The only major problem is one point you make towards the end, in your penultimate paragraph. You said that 'Antarctica remains the world's last unknown continent'. What did you mean by that?

Alex: Well, um, we don't really know very much about it. Just that it's very cold.

Tutor: But that's not really true, is it? There are dozens of scientific bases there, with thousands of scientists collecting data. What you said was true 100 years ago, but not now. A huge amount of information has been collected about what's both above and below the ground there.

Alex: Yes, I hadn't really thought about that. I know, for example, a company called ESSCOM has been exploring for oil and minerals there. I read about it recently.

Tutor: Well, that's true, but it's not really what I was thinking of. Mostly, there's been a lot of research into climate change, some of it done by this university, in fact. Some regions there have been studied in much more detail in that respect than most places in Europe and America.

Alex: Yes, of course. I hadn't really forgotten about the scientific exploration angle. I suppose I just meant that there are large areas that have never been visited by people.

Tutor: There are, of course, but it's all been closely mapped by satellites. We know what's there, even if nobody has seen it with their own eyes.

Alex: So did I lose marks for that?

Tutor: Well, to be honest, yes, a little. But don't worry too much about that one small point. In general, it's a good piece of work for a first semester. Well done. And I look forward to reading the next one.

Alex: OK, thanks very much.

It's not only natural changes and local residents' activities affecting the water supply. Few tourists used to venture into this inhospitable region, but an ever-increasing number of camel-trekking adventure tours and the like are bringing in more and more visitors. Their demand for water has put even more strain on an already fragile ecosystem. Some Western tourists use more water in two weeks than a Saharan resident uses in six months. On the positive side, visitor awareness of these issues is increasing, and there have been several successful ecotourism initiatives. Nevertheless, far too many visitors still regard the Sahara as an adventure playground and have little respect for its local people.

Narrator: You will hear a talk by a college lecturer about an early method of printing photographs. First, you have some time to look at Questions 31 to 40.
Now listen carefully and answer Questions 31 to 40.

Lecturer: Good morning. My name's Alan Wood, and I'm a lecturer in graphic design and printing. I'm often asked by my students how it was possible to print photographs in books, magazines, etc. before the technological processes we have today were invented. Well, a number of techniques were developed, but the most successful was called 'photogravure'.

We tend to think of the mass printing of photographs as something that only became possible in the late 19th century, but in fact photogravure was developed in the 1830s by one of the pioneers of photography itself, an Englishman called Henry Fox Talbot. The original process was rather limited in what it could do, but in 1852, Talbot patented his 'photographic engraving' technique. This technique was capable of printing good-quality images of both photographs and photographs of illustrations and works of art. In fact, to begin with, it was probably more widely used for printing photos of artwork than for printing photos of people and places, because there was more commercial demand for that.

Talbot's process was refined by a Czech painter called Karel Klíč, and in 1878, he perfected a significantly improved version of the technique. This is called the Talbot-Klíč process, and is still in use today for making very high-quality prints. However, it's now only practised in a few dozen workshops around the world, and I'm sorry to say that production is in decline at the moment.

So, how does the photogravure process work? Well, it's quite complicated, but I'll give you the simplified version. To begin with, you need a sheet of very smooth metal, usually copper. You then attach the photo you want to print to this metal sheet. The next stage I don't have time to describe in detail, but it involves using acid to burn the surface of the metal. This eats into the areas covered by the darker parts of the picture more than it eats into the lighter parts. Then the acid is washed away, leaving holes in the surface of the metal. So for example, if you were working with a picture of a zebra, the black stripes would be the deepest holes in the metal, but for the white stripes, there would be no holes at all. Grey parts of the picture would be holes of varying depths. The next stage is to apply a special type of thick, oily ink to the metal plate. This has to be spread very evenly, and it's important to make sure that the ink is pushed very thoroughly into all the recesses, or 'holes', as I referred to them earlier.

When the plate is ready, a piece of paper is pressed firmly onto it. This paper must be slightly wet, so the ink goes onto the paper in a smooth way. Then the piece of paper is taken off and left to dry. If required, the metal plate can then be inked again, and another copy made. In this way, one metal plate can produce many copies.

One of these metal sheets won't last for ever, of course. If it's used for making hundreds of copies, eventually the paper will wear away the surface of the metal, and another plate will have to be made. These days, the technique is mostly used for short runs of tens of images.

Of course, this process is incredibly slow in comparison with modern printing techniques, and the costs involved are large. So why does anybody use it at all? Images made this way have a very distinctive character, quite different from images produced with modern printing techniques. The few workshops using this method today mostly use it for producing short runs of art prints, each one selling for hundreds or even thousands of dollars. Nowadays, it simply wouldn't be economical to use it for printing pages of books and magazines, as it once was.

Answer key

UNIT 1

Spotlight 1
1 1 b 2 b 3 a

2 1 for 2 in 3 at 4 with 5 on 6 as

3 1 work long hours
 2 paid by the hour
 3 job satisfaction
 4 job security
 5 career prospects
 6 physically demanding

Listen 1
1 1 Business Studies 2 lifeguard
 3 other lifeguards 4 behave badly
 5 financial institution / bank / insurance company

4 *Suggested underlining*
 both / part-time student / degree / Business Studies / lifeguard /
 swimming pool
 interesting / conversations / other lifeguards
 children / stop behaving badly / parents / angry
 pleasant / boring / well paid / degree / better
 financial institution / bank / insurance company

Spotlight 2
1 1 a 2 Both are good. 3 b 4 Both are good. 5 a

2 1 lived 2 seen 3 been thinking 4 lived 5 been looking for
 6 stayed 7 found 8 been hoping

3

house/flat	area/neighbourhood
fourth-floor	commercial
rented	multicultural
shared	residential
spacious	rural
three-storey	suburban
two-bedroom	urban

4 1 multicultural 2 spacious 3 commercial 4 rural 5 shared
 6 suburban

5 1 lift BE / elevator AE
 2 apartment AE / flat BE
 3 ground floor BE / first floor AE
 4 sidewalk AE / pavement BE
 5 crossroads BE / intersection AE
 6 main road BE / highway AE
 7 downtown AE / town centre BE

Listen 2
1 3, 4 and 5 are true.

Check and challenge
Talking about your occupation
1 salary 2 job satisfaction 3 freelance
Talking about your place of residence
1 residential
2 ten-storey
3 My apartment is on the first floor, next to the elevator.
Grammar for talking about your personal circumstances
Sample answers
1 My family owns a chain of opticians, and I run one of the
 branches.
2 I'm studying Chemistry at the local university.
Collocations
1 in 2 as
Pronunciation
I live with my <u>parents in a</u> flat on the <u>top floor</u> of a <u>15-storey</u>
<u>building</u>, not far from the <u>city centre</u>.
words run together: *parents in a, flat on, floor of a*

UNIT 2

Spotlight 1
1

can follow *go*	do not normally follow *go*
camping	gardening
ice skating	playing computer games
mountain climbing	playing football
running	reading
skiing	walking the dog
walking in the countryside	watching TV

2 1 seeing 2 to see 3 to go 4 playing 5 to buy 6 to have
6 1 e 2 g 3 c 4 b 5 f 6 a 7 d
7 1 go for a 2 have fun 3 sit back 4 have some time off from
 5 let my hair down 6 relax with 7 taking it easy 8 unwind

Listen 1
1 1 C 2 A 3 B 4 B 5 C

Spotlight 2
1

music	film	book
classical	action	detective
dance	comedy	horror
independent	documentary	humorous
jazz	horror	literary
pop	independent	non-fiction
reggae	low-budget	reference
rock	science fiction	science fiction
urban	thriller	thriller
	western	western
		biography/
		autobiography

(Other uses are possible in certain contexts.)
2 1 science fiction 2 documentary about pop/rock music
 3 film about a person's life 4 romantic comedy
 5 very low-budget
3 The context and tone of voice can affect the meanings.
 Suggested answers: 1 2 2 1 3 3 4 5 5 1 6 5 7 4 8 1 9 3
 10 1

Exam skills 2
1 *Suggested answers*
 1 4 (It uses good vocabulary and grammar (*used to*), but doesn't
 go into very much detail, and the sentences are quite short,
 lacking connecting grammar.)
 2 2 (It's a reasonably detailed answer, but the language used is
 simple.)
 3 3 (The use of *used to* is good, but the sentences are very short,
 and the grammar in general is quite simple. The vocabulary is
 quite good (*important role / latest releases*), but could be more
 ambitious.)
 4 5 (Excellent use of complex grammar, vocabulary and
 expressions (*out there, know where to start, track them down*).)
 5 2 (Plenty of detail and specific vocabulary, but the grammar is
 simple.)
2 1 say 2 catch 3 repeat

Listen 2
1 1 C 2 C 3 A 4 C 5 B
4 In longer sentences, intonation is used to divide the parts. For
 example, in *Well, my final exams are next month, so at the moment
 I don't really have any free time at the weekends or any other days*
 there is a slight falling intonation on *month*, *weekends* and *other
 days*.

Check and challenge

Talking about leisure interests and activities
Sample answers
1 I adore it. / I'm very keen on it. / I'm a big fan of it.
2 I can't stand it. / I'm not very keen on it. / It leaves me cold.
3 sit back / relax / let your hair down / unwind
4 cheap / affordable / inexpensive

Talking about things you watch and read
1 horror 2 detective 3 pop 4 biography

Grammar for talking about leisure interests and activities
1 gerund 2 *used to* 3 connecting ideas with *so*

Pronunciation
Suggested answers
1 I quite like <u>horror films</u>, but not if they're excessively <u>violent</u>.
2 I read less <u>than</u> I <u>used to</u> because I don't have very much <u>free</u> <u>time</u> at the <u>moment</u>.
3 I'd rather watch a film in the comfort of my own home than travel to a <u>cinema</u>, stand in a queue to buy <u>tickets</u> and then have to sit next to lots of noisy kids eating <u>popcorn</u>.

UNIT 3

Spotlight 1
1 1 e 2 b 3 a 4 c 5 d
Note that these definitions are simplified, and there are complex usage rules and exceptions to those rules for all these future forms.
2 1 *would/'d*; *would/'d* or *will/'ll* (It depends how likely the speaker feels it is that he/she will get a Master's degree.)
  2 *wouldn't*; *wouldn't* (Both second conditional, as it's clear the situation isn't going to happen.)
  3 *won't* (It's clear the speaker is going to apply for his/her 'ideal job'.)
  4 *will*; *won't* or *will*; *wouldn't* (Depending on whether or not the speaker intends to apply for the job.)
  5 *would*; *wouldn't* (*will*; *won't* is also possible if the speaker intends to become a teacher, but only for a short time.)
  6 *will/'ll* (*I'm sure* implies that the situation is likely.)
3 1 from 2 in 3 for 4 to 5 with 6 of
4 1 3 2 1 3 2 4 1 5 1 6 2 7 2 8 2

Exam skills 1
1 *Sample answers*
  1 However, I enjoy the work and I meet lots of interesting people.
  2 Apart from that, I think it's a great job.
  3 On the other hand, it's very well paid.
  4 Even so, I think I could do that job better than he does.
2 b, d, a, c, e
Other sequences are possible, but this seems the most likely.
Observe the structure:
  1 Description of the candidate's current personal situation
  2 Specification of the type of job he/she hopes to get
  3 More detailed description of that job
  4 Explanation of the benefits of the job
  5 'Rounding off', summarizing reasons and relating the job to the wider field of employment
3 1 It's not just treating sick animals.
  2 For example, cows can catch tuberculosis from wild animals, so every cow in the country has to be tested for it regularly. Imagine vaccinating five hundred pigs, for example.
  3 I wouldn't be happy getting up every day to go and sit in an office.
4 *Suggested answer:* 3, 4, 6, 7
(In certain circumstances, all the points could be included, but only if genuinely relevant to the instructions on the card.)

Listen 1
1 2, 5, 6

Spotlight 2
1 *Suggested answers*

very often	sometimes	not often	almost never
all the time continually regularly the whole time	every now and then from time to time	occasionally once in a while	hardly ever infrequently once in a blue moon very occasionally

Note: The frequency described can vary depending on the context and the speaker's intention.
2 1 I have to work late at the office all the time.
  2 I hardly ever have to work late at the office.
  3 I have to work late at the office from time to time. / From time to time, I have to work late at the office.
  4 I have to work late at the office regularly. / I regularly have to work late at the office.
3 1 generally 2 tend to 3 Generally speaking 4 On the whole 5 mostly

Listen 2
1 1 C 2 A 3 B 4 C 5 B

Check and challenge

Grammar for talking about the future
1 will 2 would 3 Would 4 Will

Conditional futures
I'd like to get a job with a major TV production company, but I'd have to move to the capital city of my country.

Contrasting ideas
Apart from that; Even so; On the other hand; However

Relating things to your own experience
1 experience/view/opinion 2 have (any / much / a lot of)
3 found/seen/heard/noticed 4 seen/heard/noticed/read/understood/experienced

UNIT 4

Spotlight 1
1 1 have to 2 should 3 have to 4 ought to 5 should have 6 could 7 don't need to
2 1 c 2 d 3 e 4 a 5 b
3 1 c 2 f 3 e 4 b 5 a 6 d
4 1 both 2 *do* 3 both 4 *got* 5 *do* 6 both 7 both 8 *keeping*

Exam skills 1
1 1 d 2 c 3 b 4 a
2 *Suggested answers*
  1 … and thirdly, it's a good idea to …
  2 A third good idea is to …
  3 And one more thing is to …
  4 … and (c) don't forget to …
3 c, a, f, b, e, d
Other sequences are possible, but this seems the most likely.
Observe the structure:
  1 Introduction to the subject of talk
  2 The main point about why the teacher was special
  3 First reason why the lessons were special
  4 Second reason why the lessons were special
  5 First reason why the teacher influenced the candidate
  6 Second reason why the teacher influenced the candidate, plus concluding remark
4 One of the best <u>things</u> about her lessons was …
<u>Another</u> good <u>thing</u> about the lessons was …
<u>Firstly</u>, she made me …
<u>Secondly</u>, she showed me …
5 1 Not so suitable: you don't remember her very well, so there's not a lot to talk about
  2 Unsuitable: doesn't match the description on the card
  3 Very suitable
  4 Unsuitable: not a school teacher

Listen 1
1 1 every day 2 shy 3 confident 4 (more) friends 5 thank him

Spotlight 2

1 1 Few people believe examinations are a perfect way to measure ability, but most state education systems use them.

  2 Few people believe examinations are a perfect way to measure ability. However, most state education systems use them.

  3 Few people believe examinations are a perfect way to measure ability. On the other hand, most state education systems use them.

  4 Although few people believe examinations are a perfect way to measure ability, most state education systems use them.

  5 Few people believe examinations are a perfect way to measure ability. Most state education systems use them, though. / Few people believe examinations are a perfect way to measure ability, though most state education systems use them.

Exam skills 2

2 *Suggested answers*
  1 c 2 e 3 a 4 b 5 d

Listen 2

1 1 B 2 C 3 C 4 A 5 C

Check and challenge

Language for talking about obligation

1 We had to do it. / We were required to do it.

2 It was up to us whether we did it (or not). / There was no obligation to do it.

3 We weren't allowed to do it. / We couldn't do it.

(Other phrases are possible.)

Relating things to your level of knowledge

1 know much / a lot

2 know

3 an expert

4 a lot about

Language for contrasting ideas

1 I enjoyed my school **days, but** I didn't like the homework or the exams. / I enjoyed my school **days. However,** I didn't like the homework or the exams.

2 I enjoyed my school days. On **the** other hand, I didn't like the homework or the exams.

3 I enjoyed my school days, **although** I didn't like the homework or the exams.

4 I enjoyed my school days. I didn't like the homework or the exams, **though**.

UNIT 5

Spotlight 1

1 1 for 2 by 3 above 4 in 5 of 6 on 7 at 8 with

2 1 around 2 over 3 through 4 across 5 past 6 along

3 1 c 2 f 3 b 4 a 5 d 6 h 7 j 8 e 9 g 10 i

4 1 state-of-the art public transport system

  2 historic monuments

  3 inner city

  4 urban regeneration

  5 a lot going on

Exam skills 1

1 *Suggested answer*

Section 2: Describe the general characteristics of the place.

Section 3: Describe more detailed characteristics of the place and personal experiences of it.

Section 4: Summarize the previous sections.

2 It seemed; I imagine; I'd guess; I get the impression; The overall impression I have is; it seems; maybe; there doesn't appear to be

3 1 seems 2 appears 3 me 4 impression 5 I imagine 6 I'd guess 7 overall; have 8 the feeling

4 1 O 2 F 3 F 4 O 5 F 6 O 7 O

5 1 good advice 2 bad advice (It will take too long and waste valuable time.) 3 good advice 4 bad advice (The important thing is that you have plenty to say about it. But if the instructions say city, it must be a *city*, even if it's a small one.)

6 *Suggested answer*

Best topics: 1, 2, 4, 7

Listen 1

1 A, D

2 1 F 2 C 3 A

4 1 She chose a small city, but made sure the examiner knew it really was a city.

  2 She explained the reasons for the limits of her knowledge and talked about her impressions.

Spotlight 2

1 1 c 2 a 3 d 4 b

2 1 is; is 2 is; won't be 3 were*; would be

  4 had been; wouldn't be / wouldn't have been

  * In second conditional sentences, *if* + *be* always becomes *if* + *were*, never *if* + *was*. This rule should always be followed in formal English, but is often ignored in informal English.

Exam skills 2

1 1 By that I mean 2 I'm not saying

  3 In other words / To put it another way

Listen 2

1 1 A 2 C 3 C 4 A 5 B

Check and challenge

Prepositions

1 *On a bus* describes the experience of the journey; *by bus* distinguishes it from other forms of transport.

2 *Over the river* means crossing it, probably on a bridge; *along the river* means a journey from one point on the river to another, usually without crossing it.

3 *He lives in a street* means he lives in a house or flat in a street; *He lives on the streets* means that he is a homeless person.

Describing impressions

Suggested answers

1 You get the feeling that it's a city with a very bright future.

2 I get the impression that the traffic has got worse recently.

3 It's safe to walk around at night, in my opinion.

Conditionals

1 If more roads are built, traffic will increase to fill them.

2 If more roads were built, traffic would increase to fill them.

3 If more roads had been built, traffic would have increased to fill them.

Sentence 1 implies that it is likely or at least fairly possible that more roads will be built.

Sentence 2 implies that it is unlikely, very uncertain or impossible that more roads will be built. It could also imply that the roads being built depends on the approval of the other person, which is not assumed.

Sentence 3 implies that at one point it was possible that more roads would be built, but it is not possible now.

Clarifying language and **Personally,** *...*

1 In **other words**, it's a really good place to live.

2 By that **I mean** I didn't particularly enjoy my visit.

3 To put it **another** way, it's an interesting place, but it can be exhausting.

4 I'm **not saying** that I wouldn't want to visit it again some time, though.

UNIT 6

Spotlight 1

1 *Sample answers*

  1 I think [programme A] is a lot more interesting than [programme B].

  2 I think [programme A] is a bit less original than [programme B].

  3 [Programme A] is even better than [programme B].

  4 In my opinion, [programme A] is not quite as believable as [programme B].

2 *Sample answers*

  1 *The Simpsons* is possibly the most famous cartoon series of all time.

  2 That film is probably the least funny comedy I've ever seen.

3 1 a 2 f 3 d 4 i 5 j 6 c 7 b 8 h 9 g 10 e

4 1 series 2 episode 3 cast 4 dubbed 5 subtitles 6 programme 7 season 8 reality

5 1 series 2 viewers 3 audience 4 channels
5 aerial/antenna; Satellite
6 1 watch 2 see 3 view 4 look

Listen 1
1 1 satellite (TV/television) 2 English subtitles / subtitles in English 3 records 4 more sophisticated 5 less funny / not as funny
4 2, 3, 5

Exam skills 2
1 1 c 2 d 3 a 4 b 5 e
2 There are far too many advertisements as well. On some channels, they take a half-hour programme and make it up to an hour with advertisements ...
Some habits have changed too. For example, young people drink more alcohol than their parents did.
Some other sentences could also be loosely interpreted as amplification.

Listen 2
1 1 main 2 variety 3 B 4 C 5 C
2 *Suggested answers*
  1 I've often thought a̲bout moving to a̲nother i̲nternet pro̲vider.
  2 My bro̲ther works a̲s a̲ news reader fo̲r a̲ local te̲levision cha̲nnel.
  3 I'd love to̲ be a̲ famous acto̲r earning millio̲ns o̲f dollars per film.

Check and challenge
Comparative and superlative statements
1 c 2 b 3 a 4 e 5 f 6 d
Pronunciation: the schwa sound
Suggested answers
fa̲milia̲r, e̲nte̲rtainme̲nt, o̲riginal, te̲levi̲sion, te̲rrestrial, i̲nto̲nation, co̲nve̲rsation, pro̲vider
(The exact use of the schwa sound depends on the speaker's accent and speaking habits.)

UNIT 7

Spotlight 1
1 holiday resort 2 high season; low season; out of season
3 city break 4 package holiday 5 gap year

Listen 1
1 1 by car 2 big, sandy 3/4/5 C, D, F (in any order)

Spotlight 2
1 1 recently 2 while 3 few 4 other 5 couple 6 just 7 long
2 *Suggested answers*
  2 You have to book accommodation a long time in advance.
  3 You shouldn't take a car into the city centre.
  4 You can use an international credit card to pay for most things.
3 1 She said (that) she wasn't very happy with the hotel.
  2 He said (that) he could read a bit of the local language, but (that) he couldn't communicate.
  3 She said (that) she didn't want to eat in international chain restaurants.
  4 They said (that) they went there / came here every year.
  5 They said (that) they'd been going there / coming here for the last ten years.
  6 They told me (that) they'd never been there/here before.

Exam skills 2
1 1 b 2 c 3 a 4 d 5 e
2 *Suggested answer*
  1 c 2 a 3 d 4 f 5 b 6 e

Listen 2
1 1/2/3 B, C, F (in any order) 4 A 5 B

Check and challenge
Talking about past experiences
Suggested answers
1 I went camping not long ago.
2 I went camping a few weeks ago.
3 I went camping the other day.
The impersonal **you**
Sentences 2 and 3
Reported speech
1 When we arrived at the hotel, my wife **said** she **wanted** to go for a swim.
2 The receptionist **told** us that the swimming pool was closed.
3 I **asked** t̶o̶ the receptionist when the swimming pool **would** be open again. (*Although* will *is possible in some contexts.*)
4 He **told** t̶o̶ me he didn't **know** the answer.
Speaking strategies
1 philosophical 2 Expand 3 limitations 4 short; longer
5 hypothetical 6 anecdote 7 the media 8 debate 9 rule

UNIT 8

Spotlight 1
1 1 f 2 d 3 e 4 a 5 c 6 b
2 1 a 2 b 3 a 4 a 5 c 6 b 7 e

Predicting and practising 1
2 1 Gerard Ozeville 2 16A, Aston Street, Ilfracombe EX34 9GW
  3 01272 863990 4 4893 9607 6220 4554 5 11/19
  6 16th July to 21st July 7 standard double 8 €42 9 €29.50
  10 €34.50 11 7.30 (p.m.)/19:30
4 1 Adderstone 2 LE2 6HV 3 07488 269010 4 13/thirteen
  5 11th 6 10.30 a.m.

Predicting and practising 2
2 1 bicycles (and) cameras 2 (a) one-bedroom flat
  3 near (the) office
4 1 Wildlife Park 2 (public) car park 3 (a) packed lunch
  4 (exact) return time
5 1 True
  2 False (You can write one, two or three words with no number OR you can write one number plus no word, or one number plus one, two or three words.)
  3 True (Sometimes more than one answer is possible. But be careful – this only happens occasionally.)
  4 False (Any format can occur in any section.)
  5 False (All sections of the Listening test are played once only except for a short first extract of Section 1, which is played twice to give an example and to help you understand the test format.)
  6 False (You have some time at the end of the complete test to transfer your answers to the final answer sheet.)
  7 True

Preparing to answer 1
1 1 a price (in dollars) 2 a frequency / length of time
  3/4 a length of time 5 a time period
2 Instructions for getting a pre-booked taxi at an airport
3 1 fifteen dollars / $15 / 15 dollars 2 (one) hour / 60 minutes
  3 45 minutes/mins 4 20 minutes/mins 5 24 hours
  6 10 p.m./22:00 7 (your/the) plane/flight lands
  8 Airport Taxi Service (*capital letters not required*)
  9 booking reference number
  10 info@ercancars.com (*also acceptable*: info at ercancars.com)

Spotlight 2
1 1 into 2 come 3 past 4 *both possible* 5 *both possible* 6 over
  7 at 8 *both possible*
2 1 enter via 2 runs alongside 3 is divided into 4 adjoining
  5 is on the far side of 6 leading from 7 away 8 nearby

Predicting and practising 3
2 11 E 12 F 13 C 14 A 15 D

Preparing to answer 2
1 1 an event 2 more options than questions
2 1 more questions than options
  2 the relative cost of certain items
3 11 D 12 C 13 E 14 F 15 B 16 C 17 B 18 A 19 A
  20 C

Check and challenge
Writing and saying names, dates, times, numbers, etc.
Sample answers
1 March the thirteenth, (the) thirteenth of March, March thirteenth
2 13th March, March 13th, March 13, 3/3
3 ten to seven, six fifty, ten to seven in the evening
4 6.50, 6.50 p.m., 18:50
(Some other variations are also possible.)
The exam format
1 F (only once)   2 F (always two speakers)   3 T   4 T
5 F (You will usually lose marks for this.)   6 F   7 T

UNIT 9

Spotlight 1
1 *Suggested answers*
1 **Examinations** are for official qualifications; **tests** can be set by a teacher or school
2 **Grades** are often letters and can be for an essay; **points** are always numbers, usually out of a possible total.
3 English Literature is **a subject**; 'Autumn 2013: The campaigning novel, 1840 to 1875' is **a course**.
4 A **tutorial** is a discussion between a student and a teacher/lecturer; **an interview** can be for a job or a place in a college/university.
5 A **teacher** teaches in a school; **a lecturer** teaches in a college or university.
6 You **teach** a subject; you **train** people to do something.
7 **An essay** is shorter than **a dissertation**.
8 **Evidence** supports an **argument**.
9 You **pass** an exam; you **graduate** from a college or university.
10 A teacher **marks an essay**, perhaps to give it a grade; anybody can **check an essay**.
11 In **a lecture**, one person speaks to a group; **a seminar** is a group discussion, usually with a leader.
12 A **graduate** has completed his/her degree course; **an undergraduate** has not yet finished.
13 A **professor** is a very senior type of lecturer; **a tutor** is anybody who usually teaches individuals rather than classes.
14 If something is **academic**, it is concerned with study in colleges and university; if it is **educational**, it is concerned with schools and learning in general.
15 A **Master's degree** is an advanced degree from a college or university. **A postgraduate degree** is an advanced degree taken after a first degree.
16 A **discussion** can be about anything in any context; **a debate** is a discussion of an issue, often a contentious one; **a talk** is similar to a lecture, but not in an academic context.

2 1 examinations 2 academic 3 grades 4 seminar 5 marking 6 course 7 teacher-training 8 dissertation 9 tutor 10 evidence; argument

3 1 go over 2 dropped out 3 fill out/in 4 leave out 5 hand; in 6 picked; up 7 work out 8 catch up 9 fall behind 10 handed back

Focus on formats 1
2

Anna: Hi, Tony. It's great that we're allowed to collaborate on this project. It'll be much better than working on it individually.
Tony: Absolutely. And there's going to be a lot of data to process here. It's going to take hours, even with two of us. <u>I don't think somebody working alone could do it in the time.</u> *[information to choose A, the correct answer]*
Anna: <u>Would it be easier</u> to work on all of it together, or take half each? *[temptation to choose incorrect answer B]*
Tony: Well, it would be more interesting to <u>work on all of it together,</u> but it would be quicker to do half each, and we don't have a lot of time. *[temptation to choose incorrect answer C]*

3 B, D

Spotlight 2
1 NS 2 D 3 A 4 D 5 A 6 NS 7 D 8 NS 9 D 10 D
(These answers reflect typical usage. Other usages may be possible, depending on the context.)
Preparing to answer 1
2 21–23 B, D, F (in any order)
  24 B
  25 A
  26 (the/his) penultimate paragraph
  27 data/information
  28 oil and minerals / oil, minerals / minerals and oil
  29 climate change
  30 by satellites / from space

Spotlight 3
1 Academic: 3, 6, 7, 8, 9
Informal: 1, 2, 4, 5
2 *Suggested answers*

formal/academic	informal
consists of	boss
founded	doing a degree
governed by	I think
institution	lots of
known as	really good
principally	stuff
specializing in	
substance	
undoubtedly	

Spotlight 4
1 To begin with
2 The next stage
3 After that
4 Prior to
5 The end result

Focus on formats 2
1 *Suggested underlining*
This theory says that at various points over geological time, <u>the temperature of the Sahara region falls relatively fast</u> (*31*). Of course, in geological terms, 'fast' means over thousands of years. This allows <u>greater rainfall</u> (*32*), leading to so-called 'Green Sahara' periods. Those are periods when the region is covered in vegetation. However, the same process continues, and <u>temperatures then start to go up again</u> (*33*). Of course, this means that <u>the region starts to dry out</u> (*34*) and eventually reverts to desert, ...
Answers
31 (The) temperature 32 Rainfall/Rain 33 Temperatures 34 dries out
2 35 visitors/tourists 36 water 37 increasing / rising / going up 38 local people / inhabitants / residents

Preparing to answer 2
2 31 photography
  32 (photographs of) illustrations
  33 a few dozen
  34 in decline / decreasing / going down
  35 (A/The) photo/photograph
  36 acid
  37 deepest holes/recesses
  38 (Slightly) wet / Damp
  39 B
  40 B

Check and challenge
Talking about past experiences
Suggested answers: test, essay, dissertation, examination, tutorial
Academic English
Suggested answers
1 The college was founded in 1920.
2 The structure of this essay is not very good.
3 The courses are great.
4 I think the school-leaving age should be put up.
The exam format
1 F 2 T 3 F 4 T 5 F 6 F (only in Section 3)
7 F (ten minutes)